MW00364400

PRAISE FOR *RELENTLESS*

"When it comes to overcoming aphasia, Ted W. Baxter wrote the book. *Relentless* is a heartfelt lesson in perseverance, triumph, and transformation."

—JULIA FOX GARRISON, speaker and author of *Don't Leave Me This Way (or When I Get Back on My Feet You'll Be Sorry)*

"I know what it feels like to lose everything because of a stroke, and I recognize Ted's determination to make as complete a recovery as possible. *Relentless* is an inspiring story that I hope encourages others to approach their own recovery with the same resilience."

—KEVIN SORBO, actor, director, and author

"In *Relentless*, author Ted Baxter survives an extensive stroke and devotes himself to making the fullest recovery possible. This process is truly remarkable. Mr. Baxter's focus, motivation, and successful reestablishment of neurological function are a testament to the human spirit. By accessing the best available clinical expertise and rehabilitation programs, the author is able to begin a new life in which he dedicates himself to helping others. *Relentless* conveys two important messages. First, the human brain is extraordinarily plastic—it has the ability to use inputs (rehabilitative, among others) to make new circuits that make new functions possible. Second, there is a clear need for us to be able to identify individuals who are at the greatest risk for a stroke after a mini-stroke (transient ischemic attack) or for secondary stroke. This latter unmet need is a problem that modern science and medicine must address in order to reduce the prevalence of stroke and its lifelong impact."

—HOWARD J FEDEROFF, MD, PhD, professor of neurology, and former dean, University of California, Irvine, School of Medicine

"Ted's inspirational story about his recovery from a near fatal stroke is extraordinary. His force of will through a combination of courage, determination, and unrelenting resilience in the fight back from those earliest days to where he is now is profoundly inspirational."

—GERALD BEESON, chief operating officer, Citadel

"I have known Ted since almost the beginning of his remarkable aphasia journey. His persistence and steadfastness in pursuit of regaining his life is inspirational, and his story needs to be heard. Throughout his recovery, Ted has maintained his grace, his good humor, his concern for others, and his broad interests. I am honored to have learned from him. His book will serve as a model for others who have had their lives touched by this devastating problem."

—AUDREY L. HOLLAND, PhD, regents professor
emerita, University of Arizona

"Nearly 800,000 Americans suffer a stroke each year, and those lucky enough to survive are often left with some level of disability. It's inspiring to read *Relentless* and get a glimpse of Ted's strength and determination during such an arduous time."

—ERIC HASELTINE, PhD, neuroscientist, and author of *Brain Safari*

"In *Relentless*, Ted Baxter shares his experience of recovering from a stroke and the challenges and frustrations of aphasia. His determination to not let his stroke disable him and the entire process of rehabilitation and recovery can serve as an inspiration for stroke survivors and their families and loved ones."

—LOUIS R. CAPLAN, MD, professor of neurology,
Harvard University

"*Relentless* is an astonishing memoir of a man who had everything needed to succeed in life and suddenly lost it because of a stroke. Now reenergized, relearning, and recovering, Ted shares wisdom and the pieces of his completely different, new, and improved life in this inspiring book."

—JUAN PUJADAS, retired global advisory leader and
vice chairman, PwC International LLC

"Of all the patients with stroke I've cared for, Ted is easily the most remarkable. I have never seen anyone with a stroke such as his make the astounding recovery he did. And I might also add that the title for his book is apropos!"

—JESSE TABER, MD, NorthShore University HealthSystems

"Ted's passion and determination led to his miracle recovery from a massive stroke. A truly inspiring book for everyone!"

—WENGUI YU, MD, PhD, professor of clinical neurology, and director, Comprehensive Stroke & Cerebrovascular Center, University of California, Irvine

"This book is a most personal and poignant account of suffering a stroke and experiencing the painful challenges of its aftermath. This could happen to any of us, and *Relentless* gives us deep insight into what that experience is like along with the challenges of recovery. Many of us may not be so determined (or lucky). Well done, Ted Baxter, for sharing your story with such wonderful and heartening insights."

—MARK AUSTEN, chairman of Alpha Bank, ex managing partner of financial services consulting at PWC, and director of PWC Global Board

"As an occupational therapist who has specialized in rehabilitating stroke survivors for thirty years, I must say I found Ted Baxter's memoir to be inspirational and at times miraculous. This memoir is required reading for healthcare professionals to obtain critical insights from a patient's perspective. Stroke survivors and their loved ones are sure to be influenced by Ted's resilience, courage, and motivation. This memoir is a gift to the stroke survivor community."

—GLEN GILLEN, EdD, OTR, FAOTA, Columbia University, New York City, New York

"This book is an inspirational story of the significance of daily perseverance and taking responsibility for your own future by setting incremental and achievable goals. Ted's writing is not only motivational but a useful guide to the world of recovery for stroke survivors and their caregivers."

—JONATHAN BURKE, president, Laguna College of Art and Design

"*Relentless* is a wonderful story that turns tragedy into triumph. I am very proud of Ted's accomplishments. He is an inspiration for all to never give up."

—DEAN REINMUTH, world-renowned golf coach, spokesperson, and television personality

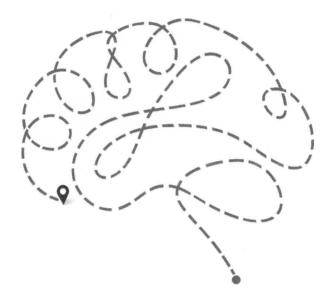

A MEMOIR

RELENTLESS

HOW A MASSIVE STROKE

CHANGED MY LIFE FOR THE BETTER

TED W. BAXTER

GREENLEAF
BOOK GROUP PRESS

The information provided in this book is based on my recollection of events and conversations to the best of my ability. Others may have different memories, and conversations may have been reconstructed. It is designed to provide helpful information on the subjects discussed. This book is not meant to be used to diagnose or treat any medical condition. For diagnosis or treatment of any medical problem, consult your own physician. References are provided for informational purposes only and do not constitute endorsement of any websites or other sources.

Published by Greenleaf Book Group Press
Austin, Texas
www.gbgpress.com

Distributed by Greenleaf Book Group

For ordering information or special discounts for bulk purchases, please contact Greenleaf Book Group at PO Box 91869, Austin, TX 78709, 512.891.6100.

Design and composition by Greenleaf Book Group
Cover design by Greenleaf Book Group
Aphasia Guide reproduced by permission of Archeworks.
©Artisticco. Used under license from Shutterstock.com
©RomanYa. Used under license from Shutterstock.com

Publisher's Cataloging-in-Publication data is available.

Print ISBN: 978-1-62634-520-1

eBook ISBN: 978-1-62634-521-8

Part of the Tree Neutral® program, which offsets the number of trees consumed in the production and printing of this book by taking proactive steps, such as planting trees in direct proportion to the number of trees used: www.treeneutral.com

Printed in the United States of America on acid-free paper

18 19 20 21 22 23   10 9 8 7 6 5 4 3 2 1

First Edition

CONTENTS

Foreword   xi

Part 1: Tragedy

Chapter 1: Four Days, Four Flights   3

Chapter 2: Hours Tick Away   10

Chapter 3: A Massive Stroke!   18

Chapter 4: Game Changer   27

Chapter 5: Can't Is a Four-Letter Word   36

Chapter 6: I'm Okay, Except I'm Not   47

Chapter 7: Not Fast Enough   57

Part 2: Early Life

Chapter 8: Relentless Since Birth   73

Chapter 9: Pedal to the Metal   79

Chapter 10: Moving, Moving, Moving: Out, Up, Everywhere   87

Chapter 11: I Wanted More   98

Part 3: Building a New Path

Chapter 12: Turning Point   105

Chapter 13: Setback . . . a Seizure?!   116

Chapter 14: I Decided to Win   120

Chapter 15: No More Limits   131

Chapter 16: Taking Charge Again   140

Chapter 17: Expanding Creativity   146

Chapter 18: Sports as My Recovery   154

Chapter 19: Life Changes   160

Chapter 20: Fresh House, Fresh Start, and Socialization   164

Part 4: Giving Back

Chapter 21: Therapy and Volunteering in
   Southern California   171

Chapter 22: Hello, Positive   178

Chapter 23: In Retrospect   183

Epilogue   187

Acknowledgements   194

Appendix A: How I Did It: The Techniques and
   Activities That Led to My Post-Stroke Recovery   198

Appendix B: Sample of Therapy Exercises   203

Questions for Discussion   209

Author Q&A   211

About the Author   215

Foreword

This book is Ted's story. Although Ted had a stroke at a young age, and this book describes his life before, during, and after this life-changing event, the story he tells is not one of sadness, of tragedy, or of negativity. Instead, it is a happy and hopeful narrative of determination, of relentlessness, of succeeding at one of the most difficult challenges of his life.

Ted compares this challenge to others in his life, from scholastic achievement and funding his own college education to building a new financial services consulting practice in Japan. Through his efforts, he finds that success has many different measuring sticks, and by the end of the book, readers will not only understand Ted's success but also gain some insight into how to harness Ted's magic potion for their own personal quests.

Ted's story is a pleasure and an inspiration to read. As a speech-language pathologist and a neurologist, we are quite familiar with stroke and the challenges of recovery. Yet Ted brings us with him on an intimate journey following a massive stroke that devastated a quarter of his brain. Left unable to walk or talk, every day was a struggle, not only for Ted but also for his wife and siblings. This book would have seemed impossible then. It stands now not only as his memoir but as testimony to the power of sheer determination.

Ted had a stroke at forty-one. Strokes (also known as "cerebrovascular accidents" or "cerebral infarctions") can come in many different forms and can be extremely severe or quite mild. Some strokes are caused by blood clots that block major arteries in the brain, others are caused by bleeding in the brain from the breakage of large vessels with abnormal walls (i.e., aneurysms), and still others by the blockage or breakage of very small vessels (e.g., arterioles). The United States Public Health Service and independent stroke support organizations, such as the American Stroke Association, have dubbed strokes *brain attacks* to make people realize that, just as with heart attacks, people with symptoms of stroke need to get to the hospital quickly. A very mild stroke (transient ischemic attack or TIA), in which stroke symptoms come and go within a few minutes or hours, is sometimes viewed as a warning sign for a subsequent large stroke.

Ted Baxter had no warning signs, no TIA. He was healthy as a horse, an avid exerciser, and took great care of himself. But he spent a lot of time on airplanes, including long airplane trips, and this requires some particular care due to the risk of deep vein thrombosis, or DVT. If you read the back of the airline magazines, they suggest exercises that will mobilize the blood in the veins of the legs and prevent the blood in the legs from stagnating and developing clots there. For most people, clots in the legs are risky because they can break loose, travel to the heart and then the lungs, and get stuck there as pulmonary emboli, or PE, which can be life-threatening. However, as Ted explains in his memoir, if the heart has a hole connecting the right side with the left side—a condition called *patent foramen ovale*, or PFO—then these clots can bypass the lungs and go directly to the brain. Ted indeed had a PFO, and that was the cause of his stroke.

The diagnosis and treatment of stroke has changed dramatically over the past several decades. Even as late as the early 1990s, the goal of a neurologist in treating an ischemic stroke (caused by lack of blood flow from a clot) was to prevent it from getting worse and to prevent any further strokes. The ability to intervene directly to undo the ischemia (i.e., to restore blood flow) was nonexistent. Several forward-thinking neurologists were experimenting with clot-busting therapies, but none were considered safe enough to apply broadly. That all changed in 1995 with the publication of two reports of clinical trials—one sponsored by the National Institute of Neurological Disorders and Stroke rt-PA Study Group and the second by the European Cooperative Acute Stroke Study—showing the efficacy and safety of recombinant tissue plasminogen activator (rt-PA) in breaking up clots and thereby reversing a stroke in progress. Since that time, if someone with an acute ischemic stroke comes to a hospital with a stroke center within a few hours (between three and four and a half hours, usually), they can receive advanced therapy to undo the stroke. For hemorrhagic strokes (those involving bleeding in the brain rather than clots), such stroke centers can also intervene rapidly.

Ted's stroke was in 2005, at about the time that hospitals were beginning to become certified as stroke centers. Much of the national and regional infrastructure for advanced stroke care was not yet in place, although many of the top hospitals in the country were already developing such programs. Nevertheless, Ted did not receive rt-PA, and he developed significant damage to his brain. On this score, Ted is not unusual. Stroke patients who have received rt-PA have wide-ranging effects from the brain injury. It is hard to predict the benefits of rt-PA for an individual stroke patient, but receiving it earlier is better.

Although stroke risk and incidence increase with age, a stroke can occur at any time, even before birth. About 795,000 Americans will sustain a stroke this year, and many will be left with deficits in walking, talking, and other skills (e.g., using a dominant hand). Stroke is the leading cause of long-term disability in the United States and in many parts of the world. The most rapid phase of recovery occurs in the first six months, and subsequent gains are much slower and harder to achieve. Most people with strokes will not have as much recovery in the months and years after stroke as Ted Baxter, and as a result, we cannot underestimate the value of Ted's messages of perseverance and determination.

One of the major manifestations of stroke is a difficulty communicating with speech. This disorder of speech and language following stroke, also accompanied by problems of memory, is called *aphasia*. It's surprising how few people are familiar with this term, given that the disorder currently affects as many people in the United States as Parkinson's disease—over a million Americans. From the Greek, meaning "without speech," aphasia is far greater than lack of speech. It is a disruption of the entire brain system by which we communicate and understand meaning using abstract symbols, such as spoken and written words, signs (in the case of sign language), or the raised dots of cells (in the case of Braille). It also affects our ability to understand how those words are put together and how to disentangle the specifics of a message from its component parts. This system in the intact brain relies on complex interactions, still poorly understood, among many collections of neurons, or brain cells. The left hemisphere of the brain plays a large role in understanding and producing speech sounds and single sentences, and the right hemisphere emphasizes the cadences of sentences and the understanding of longer passages. Damage to the left side typically causes far more severe problems with speech and language than the right. When a stroke affects the left side of the brain, as did Ted's, neurons that contribute uniquely to these processes may die, and with them dies the ability to talk, to understand speech, to read, and—despite the book that lies before you—to write.

Similarly, the left hemisphere contains motor neurons that control movement on the right side of the body. So, too, Ted lost use of his right arm and leg. He learned to feed and groom himself with his nondominant left hand until he was able, through months of therapy and tireless exercise, to regain his strength.

Both of us have found ourselves, at various points, unable to walk and reliant on crutches to get around. Both of us required time to heal and physical therapy to strengthen before we were able to walk again, as did Ted. Yet both of us also knew with certainty that we would walk again, and that is a crucial difference. To work hard in full knowledge that your goal will be achieved is nothing more than common sense. To work unflaggingly toward a goal that may forever elude you is something else entirely, and it is this *je ne sais quoi* that makes Ted's story so compelling. It is this quality that we ask of stroke survivors, that we wish we could prescribe, in order for them to achieve the inherently impossible-to-define goal of optimal recovery. In truth, however, neither of us believes that we, personally, would be able to fight adversity to this extent if faced with the same obstacles, even with our concrete professional knowledge that it would indisputably be the best course of action.

As is echoed throughout this book, Ted has a special trait, and a rare one. Even before we met him, he had beaten the motor deficit and was already walking, running, writing, and even golfing, using his right side as if it were always there for him. Of course it wasn't, but through hard work, extreme dedication, and perseverance, he beat hemiparesis (weakness on one side of the body). We met Ted when he was still fighting the aphasia. Incredibly, although we know that he has aphasia, it is only because of our training that we know. Many of the people he meets in everyday life can't tell. At one point, his golf instructor couldn't tell. Did he have weakness? No. Could he walk? Yes. Did he have a mental disability? No. As far as he was concerned, he was fine.

Indeed, despite his aphasia, which is getting better day by day, week by week, and month by month, Ted gives public lectures. He does advocacy work—using language—for stroke care and research. He holds fund-raisers and stroke awareness seminars. During the week that we are writing this preface, Ted will be lecturing to the University of California, Irvine, medical school class of 2018 in their introductory neuroscience class. He is as determined to beat aphasia—both personally and more globally—as to achieve any of the other challenges he has faced. This bodes well for beating aphasia.

We wish that we could actually cure aphasia. We are working on it, and Ted is helping. We truly believe that if we were able to give Ted a stem cell transplant, or implant a device in his brain, or make his brain cells regenerate, he would be the ideal candidate. He would make sure to do the drills or practice the language tasks that would get the implanted or regenerated cells to connect with the others in his brain in just the right way to cure his aphasia. This research is ongoing, and Ted has been helping us work on some of the long-term plans. Within several decades—perhaps earlier—this may be a reality.

Ted is on the road to beating aphasia without the benefit of futuristic brain transplants. In our careers, we have not seen anybody beat it. Our research careers are built on developing advanced biological interventions to remedy it. But frankly, after knowing Ted and reading his personal story in detail, we don't doubt that it is possible, and we don't doubt that Ted will be the one. He is relentless. He is a great role model for all of our patients. We are thankful that he is on our side.

—Steven L. Small,
PhD, MD, Professor and Chair of Neurology

—E. Susan Duncan,
MA, MS, CCC, Speech-Language Pathologist
and PhD Student, University of California, Irvine

PART 1

-

Tragedy

CHAPTER 1

Four Days, Four Flights

I was at the top of the totem pole.

I had surpassed all others on my globe-trotting climb to the top of the financial industry. I was a man on a mission—a constant blur of motion as I steadfastly pursued my career goals.

I have a resume that would impress the best of the best. I spent years devoting nearly every waking moment to the Price Waterhouse financial services consulting group. I started and grew their Tokyo division, which led to my designation as partner.

When that challenge was no longer enough, I left Price Waterhouse and joined Credit Suisse First Boston as the regional financial controller for Asia Pacific. When they moved me back to Manhattan to serve as American financial controller and then on to global managing director of financial systems and strategy, I found myself bored once again. I needed an even greater challenge. I had to keep moving. So my wife and I relocated, yet again, to Chicago, so I could take the position of global controller at Citadel, one of the most successful hedge fund companies in the world. At forty-one, at the peak of my game, I was the go-to guy in the financial services arena.

I have an impressive resume, but it didn't come without a great deal of effort.

And in an instant, it was all gone.

I remember bits and pieces of the weeks leading up to my collapse.

For instance, I remember being impressed by the view as my wife and I landed on Mauritius, an island off the coast of Africa, en route to an all-inclusive resort. As would be expected, we were dressed for relaxation when we walked out of the airport into the bright sunshine, with sunglasses in place and shorts showing off our untanned skin. Winter in Chicago had, as usual, been brutally long. Things were starting to thaw there, but it would be another month, at least, before we had day-to-day nice weather. We were in major need of a warm getaway, and I remember the sun feeling exceptionally good, despite my wandering mind.

I was, as always, thinking about work, wondering if the last presentation had sealed the deal with a stubborn international client. Those concerns had me checking my email, via BlackBerry, as often as possible.

"What are you doing?" Kelly asked as someone had to weave around me, my nose pointed directly at the mobile screen.

"Just checking my email," I mumbled in reply, too busy absorbing what I was reading to meet her eyes.

"Don't worry about your email, Ted. Look! This place is beautiful." Though the words were true, her voice lacked its usual conviction, and that did make me take notice. I placed an arm around her shoulders, thinking that she really could use the sun. Her face was quite pale.

Then my BlackBerry beeped an alert, and my eyes were back on the small screen.

When we climbed into the back of the car that would take us the rest of the way to the resort, I looked up at Kelly again. She was resting her head against the black leather seat. I poured a drink from the decanter beside me and offered her one. She shook her head ever so slightly, turning the drink down.

"Is there a gym at the resort?" I asked, believing that conversation would help her perk up.

"Yes. You aren't going to work out this week, are you?" she replied.

"Of course I am. I always do," I answered. It was an argument that she couldn't win, so she just shook her head at me, as she often did.

"Try to enjoy the vacation, Ted."

I chuckled and slid in closer to her. "I will."

She smiled but still didn't lift her head.

"Are you okay?" I asked, feeling the warmth of the back of her head seeping into my arm.

"I'm okay. I think I must have gotten motion sickness on the plane."

I knew that wasn't the case, and so did she. We had been together for years, and in all the time I knew her, she'd never suffered from motion sickness. A fever took hold of her later that day, and she spent the majority of our time in Mauritius in bed with the flu.

Without my wife to keep me from it, I worked. That's how I was and what I did. I spent most of our trip using the resort's Wi-Fi to keep in contact with my colleagues and clients. Many were all too happy to take a trip to the African island to meet with me in person. After all, Kelly was right; the place was beautiful.

A week later, with Kelly feeling much closer to her normal self, though without the tan that she had so hoped for, we boarded a flight headed back to Chicago.

"When do you leave?" she asked as we buckled into our seats.

After taking the requested pillow from the stewardess, I turned to Kelly. "I leave Sunday. Shouldn't be gone more than four or five days." I went to Europe on business about every six to eight weeks.

"What time?"

"I'll have to check the itinerary. Overnight, though. Ten-hour direct flight to London, then on to Luxembourg . . . and I think that'll be the only other stop this time."

"That's good," she said, accepting a cocktail from the stewardess. A devious grin tugged at her lips as she looked up at me and sank deeper into the airline chair. I watched her take a sip of her drink, and then she set her hand on my arm. "It's not all bad, you know. Comfy pillows, drinks, snacks. I could get used to flying all of the time."

I laughed. "Well, it's not all it's cracked up to be, you know," I responded, leaning back a little farther in my own chair.

- - -

That flight to London on the Sunday after we returned from Mauritius was the first of four international flights that I would take in a matter of four days. The final flight of the four was the return trip from London to Chicago on Thursday. On this flight, I was exhausted, which wasn't like me, and I figured it was just the lack of sleep, jet lag, and being away from home for so long.

"Can I get you anything else, sir?" the stewardess asked after handing me the pillow.

"No, thank you. This'll be fine. Can you just wake me ten minutes before we land for a cup of coffee, please?" I said.

"Of course, sir. Sleep well." Whether or not her words had anything to do with it, I can't say, but I do know that I slept that entire flight. I didn't wake for the meal, a drink of water, or a trip to the bathroom. "Sir, it's time to wake up. Sir? I have a cup of coffee for you," she said in a sweet voice. I smiled in thanks and took a sip of the coffee. I never sleep through an entire flight.

It was Thursday afternoon, and I was checking the incoming emails on my BlackBerry on my way out of the airport when my limo driver called out to me.

"Good afternoon, sir. How was your flight?"

It was then that I noticed that I wasn't walking right. I found myself limping every four or five steps as I walked over to the limo. "It was fine, thank you."

"Are you all right, sir?"

"Yes, I'm fine. Just tired from the flight," I answered, further baffled at the fact that, despite the hours of uninterrupted sleep, it was a true statement.

The driver glanced at my leg as I got in. I guess my limp was more obvious than I thought. "Leg is bothering me. Too much time sitting on the plane, I guess," I said, rubbing it a bit as I sat in the soft leather seat.

The driver didn't say anything more, and I promptly put the thought out of my mind. There was work to do, and besides, this wasn't the first time I'd had trouble with my legs. I had long since given up on the idea of having legs free of varicose veins. I had asked several doctors about them and was always told that the noticeable veins in my legs were superficial and not the dangerous kind. Even if I had them stripped, for cosmetic reasons, varicose veins like mine usually come back anyway. Genetics at its finest.

When I arrived home, Kelly greeted me as soon as I walked in the door. "Welcome home," she said and then gave me a small kiss on my cheek before quickly returning to what she had been doing before I walked in. I watched her make her way to the kitchen. She had laid a stack of my mail on the entry table, like usual, so I grabbed it on my way to my office.

"You're not going out, are you?" she called from the other room.

"No, I'm going to get these bills paid and get stuff ready for work tomorrow."

"Do you need help getting unpacked?" she asked, sticking her head into the doorway.

I smiled and shook my head. Even though traveling was part of my routine, she always seemed excited to see me come home. "No, I'll do it. I've got to get my gym bag packed anyway."

She rolled her eyes and walked away. I knew that most people didn't work out like I did, but it was a part of my routine that I wasn't willing to part with. So the next day, like every day, I would wake up by five so I could be in the city by six. That gave me an hour to work out and a few minutes to get cleaned up before I had to be at the office. Kelly laughed at me, but she was health conscious too. We both maintained a healthy diet, didn't smoke or take recreational drugs, and drank infrequently, in moderation. Physical fitness was a priority for us in life. And for me, not only did it allow me to feel good, but it didn't hurt my image in business either. I was the picture of good health.

Except, my leg hurt.

The Stroke

When we walked out of our home an hour or so later to get some dinner, Kelly asked me about my leg. "Why are you limping?"

"I'm not limping. My leg . . . it's just a little sore." I rubbed it and made a conscious effort to walk naturally. "What do you want to eat?"

"Sushi okay?"

"Sounds great," I answered, opening the front door for her.

We arrived at our favorite local sushi restaurant in the next town over and were seated in the dining room.

"Don't you want a drink?" Kelly asked after the waiter came to take our drink order and I declined anything other than water. Typically, I would have ordered a large hot sake and enjoyed every warming sip with our sushi, as I had done when I lived in Tokyo.

"Not tonight. Just water is fine," I said.

She looked at me with a funny expression but let it go and told me about how she'd spent her time while I was away, saying once again how much she wished that she hadn't been sick on our trip. I was happy to keep up the usual stream of conversation, happy to be seated across from her eating the delicious meal, but when the bill came, I quickly pulled out my card and handed it to the waiter. I was ready to go home.

"Would you do me a favor tomorrow?" I asked Kelly as we walked through the front door of our home. "Can you call and schedule me an appointment with my doctor? Just sometime later this month, after your appointment."

"Are you all right?" she asked. Concern covered her face. "I can try to get you in sooner."

"I'm fine. It's just that my leg is sore, and sometimes it feels like I'm experiencing growing pains. The doctor will just say the same thing he always does, I'm sure. 'Don't worry about the pain. It's no big deal.' But it feels worse than usual." I rubbed my hand over it, and she agreed to make the call for me.

I made my way to our bedroom and sighed as I sank into the couch in the sitting room of our master suite. Kelly laughed and fell back in the chair beside me. "You're not going to sleep already, are you? It's only eight o'clock."

"Nah. Not yet," I said groggily, picking up a *Men's Health* magazine. I really was tired, but I flipped a few pages until I came to an article of interest. "Look, maybe I should start taking this supplement," I said, showing her the article.

"You already take a few different ones," she answered. I pointed to the list of the four supplements men should be taking. I was already taking three of the four.

The Apprentice was on, and a few minutes into the show, Kelly asked, "Did you see that commercial?"

I picked up the remote and rewound it, thinking again how wonderful TiVo was. I watched the commercial but didn't respond.

"Did you see that?" she asked again, looking to me, surprised that I didn't have a comment to make about it. "What's wrong? Don't you think that's funny?"

I didn't respond. I realized I couldn't respond. Suddenly, I couldn't get my mouth to form any words. I was extremely light-headed, and I began to shiver. I felt pain in my head like a really bad migraine but something I had never experienced before. I couldn't say anything, and nothing made any sense.

"C'mon, Ted. It was funny, and you know it. It wasn't that bad."

I didn't answer. I couldn't answer. I was too busy almost dying.

CHAPTER 2

Hours Tick Away

Kelly

I knew in a second that something was wrong. Ted had a blank stare, and he kept blinking, blinking, blinking. He was squeezing his right hand and leaning to the right.

"Are you okay? Can you breathe?" I asked him.

He didn't respond.

I grabbed the phone and dialed 911. The operator asked what was wrong. What *was* wrong? I explained to her about our night—about having just come from eating sushi, how we were watching a commercial during *The Apprentice*, and the way Ted was acting. She asked me if he could walk.

I turned toward him. "Ted, can you walk?"

He didn't answer.

The operator spoke into my ear. "Someone will be there soon."

My heart raced, but I tried to stay calm . . . for Ted, for the medics who I hoped would be there soon, for myself. I lightly took his hand. "Stay awake, Ted. Keep yourself up."

A few moments later, I ran downstairs to let the police in, and within minutes, the paramedics were there too. I explained the situation to them, but they couldn't tell me what was wrong.

They then started working on Ted. His blood pressure was low and falling. The bottom number kept dropping: 100-something over 72, something over 58, something over 40. The paramedics were asking him questions that he couldn't answer. I couldn't answer them either. My heart raced, and his blood pressure kept falling.

Every second mattered. Was he going to be okay?

— — —

The questions from the police, Kelly, and the paramedics stirred the air around me, sometimes penetrating the fog and sometimes orbiting me like the space stations circle the earth. Even when I was able to make out some words, I could only stare at the fuzzy, concerned faces above me.

"Are you okay?" Kelly asked.

I'm scared, I thought, and then her face fell out of focus and then back in. I could tell she had asked something else, but I hadn't heard her. My eyes traveled to the television screen. The scene was frozen there. *TiVo. Funny commercial. Why the hell can't I laugh?*

Kelly was asking me another question, or maybe she was telling me something. I couldn't tell. She was walking down a tunnel, and I couldn't figure out where she was going, but before I could ask, she was gone, and the room had gone dark. Dark and heavy. My head throbbed against the pressure around me. *I wonder where the Tylenol is*, I thought, but then the pain was so bad I knew it didn't matter. *Maybe aspirin would be better*. It occurred to me that I might be having a heart attack, and as I sat in my dark, silent, pressure-filled world, my mind tried to remember what the symptoms of a heart attack were.

At some point, I was back there, in the same room, with the same television, and Kelly's eyes were as full of fear as I'd ever seen them. The paramedics' words continued to orbit. A policeman came forward, through the mist, and asked me something else. I couldn't answer. I couldn't tell them what I was feeling or what had happened or that I might be having a heart attack or that the aspirin was probably in the bathroom.

I felt . . . removed. And scared. And helpless.

I felt myself being carried through a fog. I caught a glimpse of the living room, with the furniture that my wife had so painstakingly picked out when we had moved in. I saw the front door with the finicky lock that notoriously fought me and my key. I saw the flashing lights of the ambulance, but none of it made sense.

Kelly

They started an IV, but Ted's blood pressure continued to fall. The bottom number was down to 39, then to 32.[1]

I looked on, helpless, while the paramedics worked with Ted.

"If his blood pressure gets any lower, he's not going to live," one of them told me.

Luckily, a few minutes later, his blood pressure stabilized. I breathed a sigh of relief.

They put him on a gurney and carried him through the house and out to the ambulance. I followed.

- - -

Where are they taking me? I wondered. Kelly had said something to me about the hospital, but it seemed like I had been riding for so very long. *Haven't I?*

Awhile later, I found myself in what I thought was familiar surroundings. I'd been in the same emergency room—Evanston Northwestern Hospital—only two weeks before. I'd brought Kelly there when she had difficulties breathing, but it looked different through my haze. Or maybe I didn't know where I was at all. Wherever I was, I knew I was lucky to be alive.

---

1 Some experts define low blood pressure as 60mm Hg diastolic.

Kelly

Two of our neighbors, friends of ours, came outside when they heard the ambulance. I saw them as the ambulance drove away with Ted inside of it.

"Kelly, are you okay? Is Ted all right?" Concern tugged at their faces, and it took me a minute to respond.

"I don't know. I don't know what happened," I answered. I tried to smile for them, but I'm not sure it was much of a smile. "I have to go. We have to get him to the hospital as soon as possible." I got in my car and took off.

We got to the hospital, and I had to explain what happened in great detail again, just as I had when I called 911.

"Ted just got back today. He flew in this afternoon. We went to dinner, and he seemed okay . . . ," I told the doctor, but Ted's complaints about his leg kept running through my head. "He has varicose veins," I said, almost abruptly. "He mentioned his leg a couple of times today. Is that related to . . . to this?" I asked but didn't give him time to answer, because my mind was in overdrive. What was happening to my husband? "He has them checked every year. He's just been so stressed out. Who wouldn't be? Four flights in four days, and three weeks ago, we were on a flight to Mauritius. He couldn't even unwind on vacation. I was sick. He was working. The flight was twenty hours each way. Is that what it is? His legs? The flights? He's so stressed out."

The doctor didn't answer, but he wrote down what I was saying. I think he was trying to keep me calm, but the questions were eating at me.

"He's always been stressed, though. He's always flown a lot, so he's used to it . . . right? He was a managing director of Credit Suisse and a Price Waterhouse Partner. He flies all of the time."

"Does he have any allergies, ma'am?" the doctor asked, still writing. "To shellfish, to the sushi, or something else he would have been exposed to on his trip?"

"No? No. He loves eating sushi. We eat it a lot."

"Has he gained weight recently? Lost weight? Gone on a new diet?"

"No. He works out every day, always has, even during business trips." Ted was more health conscious than anyone I'd ever known.

"Was he feeling okay? Was he really tired?" the doctor asked, moving his way down some sort of patient questionnaire while I fought the rising panic.

"He was fine, except his leg was bothering him. He usually wears compression socks on flights, but we were home, so he took them off." Then I said, "Look, this guy takes better care of his body and is in better health than anyone I've ever met." The doctor smiled. He patted my hand and went on with his job.

Sounds, Not Words

At some point later that night, I knew, in fact, that I was at Evanston Hospital. The room I was in was the typical sterile stainless steel on white that was so common in hospitals. I saw the doctors and nurses in their white coats and scrubs, moving around my bed, checking monitors. My eyes followed them as they swam past me.

I heard loud voices talking over each other. *What are they saying?* I thought. It was all sounds, not words. I couldn't put the pieces together. Nothing gelled. I felt like the center of blurry turmoil, fully awake in the middle of a nightmare.

Why doesn't Kelly understand? The thought kept circling through the fog. This was important. I had to tell her. She had to understand me. I touched my chin again, doing my best to focus my eyes on her blurred face so I could give her a meaningful look. Her hands came up, and I knew it was a motion of defeat. *Why can't she understand me?*

I watched her hands fall and land on my arm. I knew they were there, because I could see them there, but the sensation was not what it should be. Her hands were so light, so much lighter than I remembered them being. I looked from my right arm, where her feather-like hand was still resting, to my left side.

I wonder if her hand would be heavier if she touched me on this side, I thought, and then I noticed the shaking. Were we having an earthquake? No. Surely, I'd feel it everywhere, not just in my right arm and leg. Yet, what other explanation was there for both appendages shaking so violently? My eyes swam a bit, fluttering, making me dizzy, but I forced them to obey me, pinning them on the arm that bounced about on the bed beside me. I had control over my eyes but had no such luck with my hand. And then, the bed started to move. I felt the feather lift away from my right arm.

No, wait! The scream echoed around in my skull, but no one heard me. Two white coats and my wife were standing so close, but they couldn't hear me yelling to them. *My wife! No! I have to tell her something . . . What am I trying to tell her?*

They placed a cup in my hand, and I looked down at it. Four small orange pills sat at the bottom of it.

"You have to take the aspirin," my wife was saying, and I was annoyed that she could speak. It was so much easier to tell someone something when you could speak . . . and when you could think. *Think.*

"Take the aspirin," she said again. So I lifted the cup to my lips and dumped the aspirin in. No water. I never could understand how people swallowed pills without water, but I did my best, forcing them to the back of my mouth with my tongue. A gulp later and the pills were stuck at the top of my throat. Coughing and sputtering, I fought to get them down or up or out. Something! But they were stuck there. I choked and gagged and tasted a strange fruity flavor, and slowly the pills dissolved away. Then the bed started to move again, and I ignored the confusion about the aspirin as I looked back to my wife. The white coats moved me past her.

Think! This time I was yelling at myself. The bed was about to roll right out of the room, and I couldn't remember what I was supposed to be saying to her. *Think! This is important.* I brought my eyes back to her face. I could see the tears on her cheek. *Why is she crying? Why doesn't she understand me? Think, damn you!*

Kelly

"You can stay here, ma'am. They'll take him down for the CT scan and bring him back here when they are done. Can I get you something to drink?"

I shook my head no.

Before Ted left, he kept touching his chin. I asked him what was wrong, but he just kept tapping his chin repeatedly. Months later, I learned it was because it had gone numb.

While Ted was gone, I called his brother.

"Hello?" The voice sounded tired and I knew I had awakened him. I felt bad for that, but I knew that he and his wife would want to know.

"Tom? It's Kelly. I'm sorry to wake you, but I . . . we . . . Ted is in the emergency room. It's okay. I mean, he's okay right now, but . . . I thought you would want to know."

"What happened? Was he in an accident? Are you all right? I'm putting you on speaker. Jeannette's here."

"I'm fine. No accident. We were just watching TV, and suddenly he wasn't saying or doing anything. He was just staring off into space, and he wouldn't respond. I didn't know what to do, so I called 911," I told him.

"What did they say? What's wrong?" Tom asked

"They don't know, but they got his blood pressure leveled out, and they took him for a scan. He's okay, but he can't talk."

"Do you need us to come?"

"No. No, I just thought I should tell you. I'll let you know what they say when they come back with him," I said, and we hung up.

I couldn't call his bosses. I couldn't get into his BlackBerry to get the numbers. *Why don't I know his passwords? I should know these things.* I fought with his phone, my hands shaking so much I could barely punch the letters on the tiny keyboard anyway. I finally threw the device at the empty bed, where it bounced and then landed with a soft thud, screen down.

Either the nurse didn't notice, or she pretended not to.

"Ma'am, the doctor told me to inform you that they have taken your husband in for an MRI scan."

The CT scan was negative, so they took him for an MRI.

All that time in the emergency room, nobody knew what had happened to him. When they brought him back from having the MRI, we went up to the CCU—critical care unit.

"Can I get you a cot, ma'am? It is getting quite late," the nurse asked me after a while. I had been sitting in the small, uncomfortable chair at his side, waiting for him to say something. He didn't. I took the cot, and I didn't leave the room once that whole night.

Around three a.m., I had to push the call button. "What can I help you with?" the nurse asked as she entered the room.

"He, um . . . he had an accident, I think," I answered.

She ignored my embarrassment. "Oh yes, I see. Not a problem. I will have one of the other nurses come in, and we'll get him cleaned up in a jiffy." She was so kind that I forgot to be embarrassed for Ted and went back to worrying. He had more accidents throughout the night. *Is it possible he's paralyzed?* I had to trust that the doctors would know what to do if so.

"Can they put a catheter in?" I asked. It was morning, I knew, but the sun had not yet risen. I don't think I had slept at all.

"I'm sorry, ma'am. We can't do that yet. We're still waiting for doctor's orders."

"Can you lower the volume on the machine so he can sleep?"

She shook her head side to side in response. She changed the bedding again and gave me a warm smile as she left the room.

Most of the night, Ted was restless. At one point, he pulled off his oxygen tube with his left hand and threw it away. I didn't know if he was able to breathe without it. I didn't know anything, and I felt utterly helpless.

CHAPTER 3

A Massive Stroke!

"How are you doing this morning?" the nurse asked. It was the next day, Friday, and doctors and nurses had come and gone throughout the night and the morning. I couldn't tell the difference between them. I could have already been visited by that same nurse hours before, but I didn't recognize her. Kelly told her that we were both doing well, but surely the dark circles around her eyes and the worry filling them told the nurse a different story. Nevertheless, likely used to similar reactions from so many others in the critical care unit, she straightened a corner of the bed, checked my vitals, greeted the doctors who came in to check my vitals as well, and then left.

The doctors entered the room and stood beside my bed. They broke the news that my condition was the result of a massive stroke.

I heard what they said, at least I think I did, but I couldn't process it. I knew the doctors were there, in the room with us. I'm sure my eyes were focused in their direction, but nothing made sense in my head.

Three weeks later, Kelly sat down beside my bed and held my hand. "Ted, do you know what is going on? Do you understand what happened?"

I didn't.

"Ted, you had a massive stroke. Your brain has suffered a major injury," she told me, both her voice and her eyes portraying the sadness she felt.

I was devastated, shocked.

"Don't cry, Ted. We'll get through this," she added.

But it was too late. I was sobbing, and I couldn't stop. I was, frankly, in total disbelief.

Kelly

That first night, Thursday night, when they took us out of the emergency room and put us into CCU, Ted was moving his legs and arms.

"Why are you doing that, Ted?" I asked him. He kept hitting his right leg with his right fist. He was pounding on his thigh with his right fist. "What are you trying to tell me?"

He couldn't talk.

By the time the sun came up Friday morning, Ted wasn't moving at all. He was conscious but not responding.

Some techs came in to do an EEG.

"What are you doing?" I asked, concerned, as they put a strobe light directly in Ted's face.

"We're trying to induce a seizure."

I didn't understand, but Ted was so out of it that I could tell he didn't even see the flashing light.

- - -

I stared at Kelly. I knew her. I knew that I should know her. *I can't remember her name.*

"Ted, it's Friday. How are you feeling?" she asked me. It was a weighted question. She didn't expect an answer, surely, but she was undoubtedly hoping that I would suddenly find the power to respond.

What is your name? I wanted to ask, but of course, I couldn't.

When the doctors came in, she looked away and so did I. They put IVs and syringes in my veins, but I couldn't feel them. In fact, I had no idea why they were doing it. I did know that the woman beside me, even though I couldn't remember her name, looked worried.

"You were right, Ted," Kelly told me weeks later, when I remembered her name and could process what was happening around me again. "It was your leg. The doctors, they told you not to worry, but you were right to question them. The doctors said the stroke was incident induced. It was caused by a blood clot. Deep vein thrombosis formed in your shin, and the clot got to your heart and then to your brain."

> "For most people, clots in the legs are risky because they can break loose, travel to the heart and then the lungs, and get stuck there as pulmonary emboli, or PE, which can be life-threatening. However, if the heart has a hole connecting the right side with the left side—a condition called *patent foramen ovale*, or PFO—then these clots can bypass the lungs and go directly to the brain. Ted indeed had a PFO, and that was the cause of his stroke."
>
> —Steven L. Small, PhD, MD, professor and chair of neurology, and E. Susan Duncan, MA, MS, CCC, speech-language pathologist and PhD student

— — —

"You're very lucky, Mr. Baxter," one of the doctors told me that Friday morning as he took my vitals. I wasn't sure that I agreed. As my brain cleared, I realized that I wasn't myself. "If the clot had gone to your lung instead of your brain, it would have caused a pulmonary embolism. You probably wouldn't be with us at all."

I didn't die. That's true. Of course, I also later learned that if the clot had dissolved after lodging in my brain, blood flow would have been restored, and a lot of the damage would have repaired itself. But the clot didn't dissolve. As the blood flow was cut off from more and more parts of my brain, more and more of my brain cells died.

Kelly

In addition to the news about the stroke, that Friday morning brought a phone call from the founder and CEO of Citadel, Ken Griffin, who was notified immediately early Friday morning by Ted's boss and Citadel's CFO, Gerald Beeson. I had left a message with the chief legal counsel at Citadel, Adam Cooper, late the night before, as soon as we had gotten settled at the hospital. I had only met Ken Griffin once, two weeks before, at a dinner.

I had been sitting in Ted's room, staring at him between the carousel of nurses ever coming and going, and then, suddenly, I was talking to the CEO of Citadel, a powerful man in the business world, to be sure. He was powerful in other arenas, too.

I told him that, honestly, I didn't know what was happening to my husband.

"I would like to call you back later today, Kelly, for an update. Can I do that?"

"You'll have to call the hospital, unfortunately. My cell phone is dead. I don't have a charger . . . or anything, really, with me."

"Let me see what I can do for you," was all he said, and then he hung up.

Within forty-five minutes, a driver from Citadel brought me a cell phone.

And then shortly after that, an unfamiliar man dressed in the typical white doctor's coat walked through the door of Ted's hospital room.

"Hello, Mrs. Baxter, Mr. Baxter," he greeted us, never leaving Ted out, despite his obvious inability to respond. "I am Dr. Jesse Taber, a neurologist with the hospital."

Dr. Taber was absolutely fantastic: kind, compassionate, able to explain things. Ted and I would, even years later, consider him the best neurologist we saw. He never cut me off and always took the time to listen to me, even when I couldn't get my points across to him precisely because of my emotional state. He knew enough to reply to me when I asked a question or made a comment. We were fortunate to meet with him.

"I think it would be a good idea to move you to the ICU, Ted," Dr. Taber said, and that is what happened.

All because Ken Griffin made a phone call.

- - -

Since a stroke is a brain injury, there's bruising and swelling, like with any injury. When older people have a stroke, the swelling is less of an issue because the brain naturally shrinks with age. There's room inside the skull for the brain to expand after the trauma of a stroke.

I was only forty-one. I was young. There was no place for the swelling to go.

"This is what you can expect over the next several days," Dr. Taber told my wife that morning. I wasn't there. At least, I wasn't functioning enough to comprehend where I was or what was happening. So, I wasn't able to hold her hand or provide her comfort while she received the devastating news.

"Basically, his brain will swell. The stroke was a massive one. It did some major damage. The swelling will add pressure on the brain stem, where all the bodily functions are handled, and there is a significant risk his body will begin to shut down. His heart will stop, his breathing will stop—everything will stop—and he will die."

Kelly

As Dr. Taber spoke, my body went rigid. "What are the signs?" I asked. My world was being ripped apart. My husband was dying, but it was like my body wasn't aware of it, and I sat tall and straight as I spoke with the man who was the bearer of such horrible news. "What are the signs . . . the signs that his brain is swelling?"

He was a doctor. He'd probably delivered the same news to dozens or even hundreds of other families, simply because of the line of work he had entered into. Yet, he wasn't cold or detached. He was kind with his delivery. He handed me a tissue.

"As the swelling spreads, he'll probably run a fever. He'll have more and more trouble breathing on his own. He'll sleep a lot."

"But, he's already sleeping. He's already sleeping so much." *What will sleepier look like? Will I know?*

I sat there thinking that my husband would probably die. I panicked every time he kicked or threw the covers off with his left leg or arm. He had no movement in his right side. The doctors had told me that he wasn't seeing out of his right eye. My husband, who had taken such amazing care of himself throughout all the years we had been together, was lying in bed, deteriorating before my eyes.

I made a call on my phone. "Tom, it's Kelly."

"How's he doing?" You could tell he knew things had gotten worse. I couldn't hide the worry in my voice.

"He's in critical condition, Tom. They, um . . . they said it was a massive stroke. Half of his body is paralyzed. I, uh . . . Tom, you better come soon, as soon as possible. They said that he . . ." My voice broke so many times on that call. The tears that I was trying so hard to fight were clogging my throat, making it tough to say anything. "Tom, he might not make it."

Gary, My Brother

I got the call on Friday morning, and later that afternoon, we were on a plane.

"Citadel sent a limo to pick us up so we can fly to Chicago on a private jet," I muttered. I climbed into the limo feeling like I was living the life of the rich and famous. And yet, we were all a bit numb.

The limo delivered us to the airport. There were, of course, other planes and helicopters not far from the one we were about to board, but one in particular caught our attention: Trump's private helicopter, in a nearby hangar.

Emotions were undoubtedly running high. It was, I think, the first time that all of us realized how important Ted's role was, how far he had come in such a professional setting.

It was so strange to be experiencing something that would, at any other time, be such a thrill, but to know that at the end of it, our brother was lying in a hospital bed, fighting for his life.

The Decision

So much had happened in a single day. I had been moved twice but was back where I had started—in ICU. Ken Griffin had called and again offered his support. Gerald came to the hospital to see how else he might be able to help. Later, for example, I wondered how my family had appeared at my bedside in Chicago so quickly when they lived in Long Island. It was those individuals who knew me well and I worked with day-to-day—Ken, Gerald, and Adam—who took care of the travel arrangements for my family. This also gave Kelly some breathing room to figure out what she should do next.

My wife had received the devastating news that, if I were lucky enough to go home at all, I would be unable to do anything on my own ever again, or I could be in a vegetative state. And, while all of this was happening, I was far too out of it to be aware of any of it.

Saturday brought another big moment in Kelly's life, in more ways than one. Not only was she told that I would likely die from the swelling caused by the stroke, but she was also asked to make a significant decision that could mean the difference between life and death.

"It is your choice, ma'am—surgery or no surgery," the doctors told her. With so simple a sentence, she was asked to make a momentous choice.

The surgery wouldn't correct any of the damage already done; it would only release some of the pressure by removing part of my skull so my brain could kind of expand out of the hole. Without surgery, my brain had nowhere to go but down. It would put pressure on the brain stem, causing additional damage and possibly death, which is what Dr. Taber had already told Kelly.

If the skull was opened, my swelling would be alleviated; the hole in the skull would release the pressure from the swelling. About four weeks after removing a portion of the skull, I'd probably have another surgery to put it back (or at least a portion of it).

I'd be alive but in little more than a vegetative state.

Kelly

I asked Ken Griffin and Adam Cooper from Citadel to come and sit down with Dr. Taber and me on Saturday morning, before Ted's family got to the hospital.

I met Ken and Adam as soon as they arrived, glancing down at my attire—yoga pants and a sweatshirt I had put on two nights ago.

I was so tired, but I knew I had to make a decision. I knew they would have significant input that would affect my ultimate decision, and I also knew that Ted would want me to consider their comments.

We sat down in a conference room, and they asked me if I wanted anything to drink before we started our conversation. I said no thank you.

"I have to know what you'd want," I said. "You guys are closer to Ted than his brothers. You share his drive, you're more like him in personality, and you love your professions as he loves his. If you knew you could never talk or walk again, that you may or may not be aware of your surroundings, what choice would you make? Would you have the surgery?"

At first, Ken Griffin didn't say a word. He was contemplating this huge life decision and really thought about it before he spoke.

"I promise, I want your honest opinion. I won't hold this against any of you. I just need someone to talk this through with me. If you were in Ted's situation, what would you want your wife to do?"

One by one, they each said the same thing: "I wouldn't want to live."

Ted and I had living wills, so I already knew that if he could, he would have said the same thing. I simply needed confirmation from someone who knew who he really was.

The surgery would keep Ted alive, but that's all it would do. It wouldn't correct anything. It wouldn't reverse any of the damage already done. The speech and physical deficits and whatever other injury he'd already suffered . . . no surgery could reverse the brain damage.

"Don't operate."

And I closed my eyes. *Whatever is meant to be will be. I'm not going to keep him alive to live in a hospital bed.*

I walked away from that meeting, found my way to the chair beside Ted's bed, and awaited his brothers and sister to break the news—the news that I could barely accept myself. My husband was going to die at forty-one years old. He probably wouldn't make it through the night.

CHAPTER 4

Game Changer

didn't know I was dying. I didn't really know anything. I knew when my wife was there. I noticed when my bosses came into the room, and I knew that my pastor's daughter was there to speak with me, but I don't remember anything they said. Did they talk to me? I tried to be alert. I'm not sure I pulled it off.

Kelly

"Don't be surprised if he doesn't respond to you. He looks around a bit but doesn't seem to understand what we are saying to him. I'm not even sure if he knows I'm there." I told this to Ken Griffin, Adam Cooper, and Ted's boss, CFO Gerald Beeson. It was true. Ted was essentially nonresponsive, except that suddenly . . . suddenly, he was different. He acted differently when these three people walked in the room. *He knows. He knows these guys.* He trusted them, and they trusted him as well. He was glad they were there, and he could hear them. I just knew it.

"Hi, Ted." Gerald was the first to speak to him. Ted perked right up at the sound of his voice. It was amazing. He looked around, and it was obvious that his brain was processing the faces of the men before him. It was the most I had seen from him in many hours. He, somehow, found the strength to put on his best show.

The men looked at me, and I smiled. I really smiled, and I meant it. It was so good to see some response from Ted. As soon as the three men left the room, I took the seat on the left side of the bed, knowing he couldn't see out of his right eye. He was kind of out of it, but he looked at me.

No, not kind of—he was completely out of it, but he looked at me anyway.

"Ted, if you had to live in a hospital bed the rest of your life and you couldn't walk or talk, would you want to live?"

He squeezed my hand.

Aw, damn it. Was that confirmation yes, he'd want to live? Or no, he wouldn't?

So I repeated, "If you had to live in a hospital and never walk or talk again, Ted, would you want to live?"

He squeezed my hand again.

I left the room and crossed the hall to call Dr. Terry Sullivan, the doctor Ken Griffin had recommended from the get-go. Dr. Sullivan really cares for his patients, and after I spoke to him, I knew he'd put me in touch with the top neurology specialists who could help with Ted's condition.

From the phone, I could see Ted. His bed was elevated just enough so that he could look around the room but not enough that it actually held him upright. But suddenly, he was upright.

As I looked at him, Ted sat up in bed.

He can't sit up. He can't sit up. He can't move, I thought. But, he did. He sat up. *You know what? He'll overcome this.*

He was letting me know, and I could almost hear him saying the words. "Yeah, I want to live, because I'm not going to be in a hospital bed the rest of my life."

Just then, Dr. Sullivan answered the phone.

"He just sat up," I said, though I'm not sure if I was telling myself, Dr. Sullivan, or the universe.

"No, he didn't do that. He couldn't," Dr. Sullivan responded.

"He just did it! I saw him! I watched it happen!"

I hung up and walked back into the room. I was so scared. Even though Ted probably couldn't comprehend what I'd asked him a few minutes before, on some spiritual level, on some energetic level, he obviously had.

And then the doctor's words, each reiterating the next, ran through my mind. "You do understand, Ted isn't going to have a normal life after this. He's going to need a lot of rehab, a lot of recovery time, maybe a full-time caregiver, and that's assuming he can actually pull through. He had a massive stroke."

But I knew that day: Ted had something else in mind.

Ted was letting me know he was going to survive.

Family Matters

A few days after the stroke, while I was still in the ICU, my brothers, Tom and Scott, and my sister, Nancy, came into my room. I think I smiled. I wanted to smile. I don't actually know if a smile was possible at that time. The emotions were clear on their faces—the recognition, the love, and the sadness.

"Is there anything we can do?" Nancy asked Kelly, which was good, because she had been dealing with so much. But it was also tough, because the visit would be short-lived. It had to be. They lived in New York. I was in a hospital in Illinois.

"I wish we could be with him, with you, through this mess," Nancy said.

"It's okay. I'm sure he's happy to see you," Kelly had told her.

My sister couldn't have known. They couldn't have known how happy I was to see them. They were there to lend support when I needed it the most.

Jeannette, My Sister-in-Law

Gina, our daughter, was a senior in high school at the time of Ted's stroke. "Mom, I want to go too," she begged.

"No, Gina. Not this time," I responded, because I didn't know what awaited us on the other end of the flight. Tom and I didn't think it was a good idea just yet.

She was close to Ted because of the many family vacations we took with him and Kelly.

"Mom! I have to be there," she said, the tears now running down her face. But I still couldn't give in, because I didn't want her to see him suffering. I didn't know what to expect.

"Listen, not this time. When we go over to see him again, we'll bring you with us."

"What if . . . ," she started.

"Don't say that. You know him. You know how strong and healthy he is," I told her. At this, we both smiled through our tears. "Get him a card and we'll mail it to him. I'm sure he would appreciate that."

Not long after that, she did send him a card, and her inscription read, "Dear Uncle Teddy, I just want to let you know that I look up to you in so many ways. I admire you so much, and your success is truly an inspiration to me. I know your strength will help you pull through this."

Nancy

Devastating. That's the best word I can come up with to describe how I felt that night.

I got the phone call at my home in Long Island.

"Who is calling at this time of the night?" I said aloud before answering in the scratchy voice of someone woken from a deep sleep. It was late Thursday night. I'd been asleep for a while already.

"Nancy?"

"Tom? What's wrong?" I could hear it in his voice. Of course, I immediately thought the worst, and I wasn't all that far off.

"Ted's in the hospital. He was taken in an ambulance earlier tonight. Kelly just called. She said they are trying to figure out what's wrong. She doesn't know much. She just said that he's okay for right now. They got his blood pressure stabilized in the ambulance."

"His blood pressure stabilized? What happened? Was he in an accident?"

"No, they were just watching TV and he stopped talking, and she knew something was really wrong."

"Should we go? Do we need to go . . ."

"I don't think so. Not yet. Kelly said that she'll call when she knows more, so we should probably just wait. Let's call the airlines and make plans for Monday."

Then, there was another call. Kelly called Tom and told him that Monday wasn't going to be soon enough. "Ted isn't going to make it through the night. His boss is sending a private jet for everybody. You need to get here now."

My son was so little at the time. I remember him watching as I raced around the house trying to pack a bag quickly. A little while later, we got on the jet. It was so surreal. Not much time passed, and we were suddenly at the hospital in Chicago.

"Mr. Baxter is only allowed two visitors at a time," the lady at the reception desk told us. "The rest of you can wait over there in the designated area. There is also a cafeteria, if you'd like to grab a snack or some coffee."

So, we paired off and went in two at a time. I went into the room with Scott, my next older brother after Ted.

He doesn't look that bad, I thought. He was awake.

"Hi. You've given us quite a scare," I told him, trying my best not to let my emotions get the best of me after the adrenaline-filled trip. Scott was putting on smiles as well. He cracked a joke, and I waited for Ted to have a great comeback. He didn't, but Scott and I laughed and continued to joke while we visited with him. He definitely knew who we were. It wasn't as horrible as I thought it would be.

I was able to hold it together there, in the room, but when we got back out to the hallway, I lost it.

"Is this the last time we'll get to see him, Scott?" I asked through my tears. I looked up and saw that his eyes weren't clear either. I had to leave the area so Ted wouldn't hear me. "You saw him smile?" I asked as we hurried away from the room.

Scott nodded. He had definitely smiled at us. He smiled.

Scott, My Brother

It's not easy to hide emotion when you are facing something like this. That's what I did. I think that's what we were all trying to do. The visit in the hospital room was rough. We joked, Nancy and I, but there was no real communication with Ted. The conversation with the doctors was worse still.

I remember hastily walking down the hall screaming in my own head, *He's gonna die! He's gonna die! This can't be happening!*

As many will do, I turned to my wife for support. I called Karen as soon as I had the opportunity to do so.

"My brother is going to die, Karen. He's going to die," I sobbed into the phone.

"Listen," she tried to console me, "he might not die. It's not 100 percent. Don't give up hope. He's very young and he's strong," she kept saying, but I had seen him. I had talked to the doctors, and she hadn't. I didn't think she knew how bad it was, but she was right about Ted being strong. The worst part of the whole conversation was the fact that she needed consoling too. She was on a field trip with our son, Bobby, and had just received a call from her brother that her father might not make it. He had been ill. She was there, crying, on the trip with Bobby, and neither of us could be there for the other.

Gary

"I'm all right," I answered, not even entirely sure who asked me if I was okay. I couldn't let him see me crying, which meant that I had to get the emotion out before I entered the room. It was all so surreal, the thought of Ted—the guy who was always so fit and active, so ready to set off on some new adventure—on his death bed. Even before I turned into his room, the reality of the situation hit me like a tidal wave. "I'm all right," I said again, but I suspected the nurse, or whoever had asked me, had already walked off. I wiped my face, fought to keep a smile there, and walked in.

He doesn't look that bad. "Hi, Ted." The words felt unnatural, but he looked in my direction. I could tell which half of his body had been hit by the stroke when I first saw him.

"Watching television?" It was a weird question to ask, but then, it is never easy to make conversation in a hospital, and it's even worse when the other person can't respond. I glanced at the screen, and there was some kind of nonsense on, nothing that Ted would like. "Here," I said, handing him the remote. I taught him how to use the remote control for the television so he could have something to do. "There you go," I said when he hit the button to change the station.

It got a little easier then, a little easier to talk to him, maybe because we had a goal to accomplish. Before long, it was time for me to leave, but I didn't feel as bad as I had when I walked in.

"You should hear what they have to say," Kelly was saying when I approached her and a group of doctors in the hallway, so we listened in on the conversation with the doctors.

"Are you sure?" I asked after they painted a picture so bleak. "I mean, he doesn't seem to be as bad as all that. I was just teaching him how to use the remote. He was doing it. He wouldn't be able to do that if this was going to kill him, would he?"

After all the angst the doctors put my wife through, none of their dire warnings came true. Nothing progressed the way they thought it would.

I did sit up in bed.

The CT scans showed that my brain *wasn't* swelling, or at least, it hadn't gotten any worse. My non-swollen brain didn't push down on my brain stem and cause systemic failure.

MRIs showed three areas of my brain had been hit, as if I'd experienced three separate strokes, but it was really only the one incident. I had the immediate damage from the stroke, and it had evolved and progressed through the night because the clot had lodged in my brain. But even though the doctors said it was unheard of, I had no additional damage from the increased swelling.

Miraculous.

Kelly

"It's just so crazy, isn't it?" I asked one of the doctors a couple of days after Ted had been admitted. They were quite familiar to me by then; I had seen them so many times. They came and went often. "Ted didn't have diabetes. He didn't have high cholesterol. He didn't have high blood pressure. He was and still is extremely strong— emotionally, mentally, and physically—but he was the one to have a massive stroke, not one of those guys chain smoking out there," I added, motioning out the window.

"That's what saved his life. He did everything right. A smoker may not have been so fortunate," the doctor replied.

What I said about my husband was true. Ted always worked out, religiously, for his entire life. When he was working full time and going for his MBA at Wharton, he didn't work out as much—maybe once or twice a week, but even that was more than what many people do. And that was the only down period that I know about. Even then, he still went to the gym, and he did some exercises at home, feeling like he was neglecting his body for the sake of his brain.

He always said, "I have to work out to stay strong, because you never know when you're going to need it."

And I always brushed him off.

But sure enough, he needed it.

‐ ‐ ‐

"Ready to try sitting up, Ted?" the nurse asked. Five days had passed since my stroke and I came to the hospital. I couldn't respond, but I was definitely ready. "We're going to swing your legs around and help you into the chair. You lean on us if you need to."

I couldn't hold myself at all really, and there was no way that I could have done it without them, but I was so pleased to be in that chair. After a few more days in ICU, I was moved back to CCU in the hospital. Soon after that, Dr. Sullivan got me transferred to the Rehabilitation Institute of Chicago (RIC). I was moved to RIC about nine days after the stroke. I no longer needed to be in an intensive care unit, but I still needed, and would for a long time, 24/7 rehabilitation.

Moving to RIC meant that at least I wasn't getting any worse. At RIC, they focused on getting my body to stabilize and function as normal as possible. They wanted me to try things on my own, like sitting, moving my limbs, and standing. I wanted to try too.

"You're sitting, Ted! You did it." Kelly would cheer me on with every new accomplishment. During that first week, I gave her plenty of reason to cheer; I took twenty steps with a physical therapist.

If I can take one hundred steps, then I can do anything. I can beat this, I told myself. I basked in Kelly's excitement in the second week, when I did just that. Somewhere in my scrambled brain, I knew that it was all up to me. My goal was to beat this—get back to 100 percent—and get back to my life. Work was waiting for me. I'd be there soon enough.

CHAPTER 5

Can't Is a Four-Letter Word

Kelly

At RIC, Ted had physical therapy and speech therapy. And within a matter of only a few days there, he was pushing past everyone's expectations.

It was unbelievable to see his progress, his determination. He battled for his recovery every day.

"No, Ted. It's the weekend. The therapists aren't here today. That means no physical therapy today," I told him.

Ted just pointed, insisting. Making noise, making himself heard, even though he couldn't speak as he once had.

"Is it okay if he goes in and uses the mats for a bit?" I asked the nurse. She looked around, almost as if she wasn't sure whether I was speaking to her.

"I'm not really sure. I . . . well, yeah. I think it'd be okay. Go ahead."

So I helped Ted get out of bed and to the physical therapy room. "All right, Ted. We're here. What do you want to do?" He, of course, didn't answer but pointed at the square stretching tables. There may not have been a therapist there to help him, but he was determined, and that meant that he wasn't going to take breaks.

Come Monday, I'd end up telling the physical therapist, "Ted spent two hours in there on Saturday and Sunday."

"What?" was the shocked response. Her head swiveled between Ted and me. I just smiled and shrugged.

"Nobody does that," she said.

"I know," I answered and laughed. Ted may not have been the same in every way, but he was definitely the same guy in that he was still as determined as anyone I'd ever known.

The therapists told him it would be okay to try to sit on the big ball to work on regaining his balance. He did crunches with his good leg up while they somehow held him.

"I've never seen anybody, Ted, with core strength like this after a stroke, or any injury," the therapist said, "or the same determination."

But that's why he was able to make this recovery. He was always prepared for the worst. I don't know anybody else like that either.

Those eight weeks as an inpatient at RIC are jumbled in my mind. It seemed like the stroke wiped out about 70 percent of my memory. And speech wasn't a focus during my time at RIC at all. They were more concerned with my body getting back to functioning properly. I, of course, was concerned about all of it. I wanted to be better already.

"Eh . . . uh . . . ? Girl!" I said, frustrated that I knew that the woman in front of me was my wife, but I couldn't remember her name.

At first, there was a touch of sadness in her eyes, but then excitement bubbled over.

"Ted, you did it! You spoke!" Her smile grew with each word she spoke. "Do you know my name, Ted? Can you say it?" I didn't really answer, but she could see that I knew who she was. She could tell somehow. "It's Kelly, Ted. Can you call me Kelly?" I couldn't.

After a few moments, I just said "girl" again, but she smiled anyway. It was something; it was progress.

"Ted, can you tell me what your password is for the BlackBerry? I need to get some information from it, for your office," she asked me.

But I simply stared at her. I don't know if I changed my facial expression, if she could see the confusion in my eyes, or if I was silent long enough that she thought to say more herself.

"Your BlackBerry?" she asked and showed it to me. I touched it, but I didn't know what to say. I didn't even know what she was asking.

"It's okay, Ted. Are you ready to go to PT?" Again, I simply stared at her. I didn't know what she was talking about. "PT, Ted. Physical therapy, like every day, the gym."

Then, I knew. I knew what she meant, and I was ready, working to get up and out of my room before anyone was there to help me. I spent as much time as I could in the therapy room, which was like a miniature Equinox or Crunch gym. They had similar equipment.

One of the nurses who was in the room came over to help me. "Hold on there, tough guy. Let's get the chair over there. Working out isn't going to do you a bit of good if you fall and hurt yourself," the nurse scolded.

I knew I had started to climb the mountain to get back to where I was before the stroke, and I needed to know that I was making progress.

The Greenfield Filter

After about a week as an RIC inpatient, I noticed my right leg, near the shin area, was still bothering me. It would hurt for part of the day, and then for the rest of the day, I couldn't feel it, which worried me. I wondered if the pain could be the start of another stroke and if those were the sensations you felt when you become paralyzed. I told Kelly about my leg, and she discussed it with one of my doctors, who suggested I have a procedure as a safety measure to prevent a stroke from happening again.

They wanted to put a vena cava filter, known as a Greenfield filter, in my inferior vena cava, in the middle of my abdomen area. The inferior vena cava (IVC) is a large vein in the middle of the abdomen that returns blood from your lower body to the heart. A vena cava filter is a cone-shaped metal device, like a basket, designed to trap large blood clots that break loose from veins in your leg or pelvis while allowing blood to pass freely through the filter around the clot. The filter would be inserted into the IVC through a small hole in a vein in my neck.

Kelly told me about this procedure and what they wanted to do, and they left the decision up to me. This was my first time having surgery like this, so I was a little leery, but I agreed to go along with the doctor's recommendation. In the end, I'm glad I had it done. It only took me out of the rehab program one day at Northwestern Hospital, and eventually, my leg stopped hurting.

Living at RIC

For the first few weeks I was at RIC, I had my room to myself. It wasn't big, but it had a window, and there was a washroom with a shower.

"Ted, let me help you get cleaned up before I go, okay?" Kelly asked one afternoon after I'd been at RIC for a couple of weeks. The nurse helped her move me to the bathroom so Kelly could wash me. Apparently, she noticed my look of appreciation, because after she had started washing my hair, she smiled. "I brought the shampoo from home. Smells good, doesn't it?" It did. It smelled amazing and interrupted the never-ending onslaught of sterile hospital smells.

The smell, in fact, is what I remember most clearly about RIC. That and the sound of fresh syringes being broken from their packaging to stick an IV in my arm, draw some blood from my arm, or give me a shot. But when she washed my hair that day, I could imagine I was somewhere else. I only heard the water running, drowning out all the rest.

"Do you want to watch the game?" she asked when I was clean and settled in the bed again. I did. I used to play basketball growing up. When my visitors left for the day, I watched the Los Angeles Lakers on the small hospital TV. I remembered the game. I remembered the rules from high school. I remembered they were in the playoffs.

I could follow the pace of it. I knew who was winning, who had the ball, and who won at the end. It was comforting.

"Is everything okay in here?" the nurse asked, just as Kelly had turned to pick up her purse. I knew Kelly was leaving, but I also knew that she would be back, and even if I didn't remember her name, that gave me comfort as well.

"I'll be right across the hall, Ted, if you need anything. The night nurses will be coming in soon, and they'll come in to say hi," the nurse said after she checked on us, and then she walked Kelly out. As much as I gained comfort from Kelly's presence, I also looked forward to being alone in the room. I wanted to get better, and I thought that I knew better than anyone else how to do that. At the time, I was still forced to use a wheelchair to get around. The nurses, and sometimes Kelly, would help me get in and out of it, but I hated it. I didn't want their help.

There were three shifts for the staff: morning, day, and night. During the day, there were maybe five nurses who checked in on me. But there were only a couple at night.

It's almost time, I thought. I might not have had the ability to formulate how to say words, but I had put together on my own that during the nighttime shift, I wouldn't be as closely monitored, and, well, as they say . . . *While the cat is away, the mice will play.* The wheelchair was close enough to the bed, and I wanted to prove that I didn't need their help to get in and out of it any longer.

Minutes later: "What are you doing, Mr. Baxter?" the nurse scolded when she found me lying on the floor. She pushed the call button, which meant that both on-staff nurses were in my room. They didn't generally like to be in the same room at the same time, because it meant that no one was available at the nurses' station. I could see their frustration, and I knew that I had blown it. I just needed a little more time. I knew I could get in the wheelchair on my own.

Stop! I'm fine! I yelled at them in my head, but they, of course, didn't hear me. *I want to do it myself. Stop!* They didn't listen.

They didn't know it, but I knew it. I simply needed time to prove it to them and to myself—I would stand up on my own, and I would do it soon. If I could get my body back, I could get it all back. I had convinced myself that 100 percent recovery was possible as long as I pushed hard enough.

But not that night. The game wasn't as enjoyable that night, with my arms strapped to the bed. I stared at the screen, frustration suffocating me.

"What happened to your face?" Kelly screamed the next morning as she rushed into the room and gently laid her hand on my swollen cheek. I couldn't answer her. *I want to walk! I want to get out of this wheelchair!* She didn't understand, and the nurses couldn't either. *I can do so much more if you'll just hear me; give me the chance.*

Not long after that incident, they moved another patient into my room.

I had been there for about three weeks and was nearly halfway through my inpatient stint at RIC.

They introduced him by name, but the name didn't register. "He will be your roommate for a while," the nurse said cheerfully. Of course, she sounded far happier than I felt about the whole situation. They did separate the room with a curtain, though, and I figured all would be fine because I could still watch my Lakers games at night. However, instead of using his own wall-mounted TV on his side of the room, he talked on the phone every night—loudly—with his mom.

"Lakers are in the playoffs," the nurse commented one evening as she made sure I was settled. Kelly had just left. "You must be very excited," she said.

I was. I was happy to see them make it that far in the season, especially because it meant that I still had something to look forward to in the evenings. My roommate pulled the curtain shut, and the nurse smiled. "Not everyone is a Lakers fan," she said and softly giggled on her way out of the room.

The game started, and I tried to ignore the loud conversation beside me, but my roommate's voice seemed to only get louder as the game got underway. Soon, he was talking so loudly that I couldn't hear the announcers. With no way to ask him to quiet down, I thought I'd give him a hint. I tried to drown out his conversation by turning up the volume. It didn't work.

Quiet! Be quiet! The screams in my head translated to mere sounds, but they were enough to be heard. From the other side of the curtain, I could hear his voice change.

"Mom, hold on a second," he said, and then, even louder still, "Hey, what are you doing?"

Yeah. Keep it down. That is what I heard in my head, though I couldn't say more than maybe ten words at that point, so what actually came out was something like, "Loud." It might have just been "Lod."

"Sorry, Mom. I'm back," he said into the phone, in the same loud tone. "No, it was my roommate. I don't know what he's doing over there. I can't understand a word."

Steep Learning Curve

The stroke had taken a lot from me. Later, after I was out of inpatient care at RIC, I returned home and had to relearn to do things—walk, talk, bathe, shave—all over again, and that meant that I made mistakes . . . stupid mistakes.

"What the heck are you doing?" Kelly asked me one day at home when she walked into the bathroom to find me shaving. I didn't answer her, but I held up the razor, thinking it was pretty obvious what I was doing.

"Ted, that's not shaving cream. It's lotion." To her credit, she was fairly patient. She didn't take the razor away from me, but she did replace the bottle of moisturizer that I had set beside the sink with a bottle of shaving cream.

■ ■ ■

A big part of the occupational and physical therapy programs, while I was an inpatient at RIC, was the group therapy element. It was important for all of us to realize that we weren't alone. It was good to know that it wasn't just me. I wasn't alone. The other stroke patients weren't all experiencing the same things that I was, but they were facing their own challenges.

I formed relationships during these sessions with a couple of guys, two patients who'd had different things happen to them. One wore a motorcycle helmet on his head; I think he'd had a bad traumatic brain injury. The other was a young guy, a college student, who was back in rehab for the second time. We couldn't have a normal conversation. None of us had the verbal capacity to do so, but another of the patients, who was quite fluent (though had obviously suffered a serious injury to his arm), was able to bridge the gap in our communication ability. With his help, I learned that my young friend had been in two serious car accidents and that he had really messed himself up as a result. I discovered that I still felt empathy for those who suffered, and I enjoyed the comradery.

That level of normalcy was good for me, because I was contending with a lot of frustration elsewhere. I couldn't read; I couldn't write. I could see the hospital signs, the elevator signs, the therapists' cards, but I couldn't understand them.

"Ted, did you hear me?"

"Ted, can you tell me what it says here?"

"Ted, are you feeling okay?"

"Ted?"

I heard my name a lot while I was an inpatient at RIC, and I knew that some of those voices belonged to the nurses. Others, I'm sure, belonged to friends. And, of course, Kelly was always there for me, but I rarely understood what was said to me, and I couldn't respond. Even if those voices were my friends, I wouldn't have wanted to see them anyway.

I understood that I wasn't the same as before. And, truth be told, the stroke hadn't only impacted my brain, my voice, my intonations, my speech, my overall communication, and my physical movement; it had beaten and battered my pride. Would it change? Would I ever be able to regain my pride and my abilities?

Although I couldn't talk to them, and while I would have shied away from the company at that point, I came to realize how important it was that I had the support of friends and family during that period. They were playing a big part in my recovery. Until I was able to speak full sentences, I didn't want to see them, but later, I came to understand that their presence and support is what I should have been focused on.

Aphasia Enters Our Lives

I couldn't have said it, and I certainly wouldn't have understood it, but my wife was becoming an expert on aphasia, which is an impairment, resulting from brain damage, of the power to use or comprehend words. She brought RIC's director of aphasia research and treatment, Dr. Leora Cherney, into my room.

"Okay, Ted, we are just going to make a short recording of your speech so we can use it as a gauge for how well you are improving," the doctor told me.

I responded, but I can't say for sure what it sounded like to Dr. Cherney.

"Remember, try to form words, but don't be frustrated if you can only manage sounds at this point."

It's rare not to be able to make sounds at all, so in aphasia treatment, any sounds are progress.

"One of the major manifestations of stroke is a difficulty communicating with speech. This disorder of speech and language following stroke, which is also accompanied by problems of memory, is called *aphasia*. It's surprising how few people are familiar with this term, given that the disorder currently affects as many people in the United States as Parkinson's disease—over a million Americans. From the Greek meaning 'without speech,' aphasia is far greater than lack of speech. It is a disruption of the entire brain system by which we communicate and understand meaning using abstract symbols, such as spoken and written words, signs (in the case of sign language), or the raised dots of cells (in the case of Braille). It also affects our ability to understand how those words are put together and how to disentangle the specifics of a message from its component parts."

—Steven L. Small, PhD, MD, professor and chair of neurology, and E. Susan Duncan, MA, MS, CCC, speech-language pathologist and PhD student

"It's too early to get him to come into our aphasia program, but I have to give him something that will help him speak. He needs a starting point, because right now, he can't even speak ten words. Let's get Ted to take a trip upstairs," Dr. Cherney told Kelly.

So they took me to a floor where the tech people were. They were trying to create a better way for people with aphasia to communicate. The device they'd come up with was like a precursor to a smartphone or a tablet that talks to you. (This was in 2005.) They showed me how to work the device, and it made sense. I've always had an affinity for playing around with technology. I was astute with BlackBerrys, but I lost that ability with the stroke, and it would be yet another skill that I would have to relearn.

"Ted, this is going to be wonderful for you," Kelly said to me, excited at the prospect. "He'll figure it out. I know it will take time, but Ted will figure this out. Can he take it with him?" she asked.

They gave me the most advanced version they had. I took it back to my room and immediately started playing with it.

The techs' instructions were in my brain, but by the time I got back to my room, I lost them. I could comprehend what they were saying when I had been in their department, but when I left them, it was gone. It was as if I had a three-minute memory.

I couldn't even express how frustrated and angry I was.

Kelly, my life . . . it'll never be the same. I'll never go back to the office.

I'll never sit in on those meetings. What am I going to do? There were many times during the recovery process when I let frustration get the best of me, and this was one of them. *What if I can never speak again?* I looked at her as the thoughts circled through my head, knowing that she couldn't hear them. *I'm going to do it, Kelly. I'm going to speak. Even if I can't accomplish it all, I'm going to do that. You have to hear me.*

Siblings

"How's he doing?" I heard the voice even before they had walked in the room.

"Better. He's getting better every day. Physical therapy is doing wonders for him."

"Can he say much yet?" I didn't hear the response, but I didn't need to. I couldn't greet him, but I was extremely happy to see my brother Jeff walk into the room. "Everyone is worried for him still." It was such a comfort to know that my family was by my side.

Perhaps it was seeing my siblings, or maybe it was the moment of revelation with the technology, but around that time, I found that my determination to recover grew by leaps and bounds. By the time that my sister, Nancy, came back to Chicago, I was convinced that my recovery was up to me. As long as I wanted it badly enough, it would happen.

"Ted, we have great news," Nancy said to me when she arrived. "The doctors are going to let you go out for the day."

"Just make sure you guys take care of him," the nurse warned, moving to help me make the transition to the wheelchair. She was obviously hesitant, but Kelly, Nancy, and I were excited.

"Where do you want to go?" Nancy asked. I couldn't answer, but Kelly could.

"How about the deli? It's not far from here." Kelly loved the place, and I liked the idea of good food. I especially liked being out of the hospital.

There was only one problem . . . I hated being in the wheelchair.

CHAPTER 6

I'm Okay, Except I'm Not

O ne month after the stroke, I was still paralyzed on the right side of my body—and in a wheelchair. As soon as I could move anything new, I forced myself to use that part of my body as much as possible. *I will walk again!* The words were like a mantra inside my head, and I said them so often that I made them come true.

"Well, Ted, we are going to miss you," one of the physical therapists said to me when it was time for me to be released from RIC. "You've done an amazing job," she added as I crossed the room with her at my elbow. I was walking. Granted, I had a notable limp, but I was walking.

Kelly was smiling when we came back to the table where she waited. I think I smiled back.

"You can take this cane home with you today, and if you need—"

"No." I didn't say much, but I said that. I pushed the cane away. I was walking, and there was no way that I was going to rely on aids any longer.

Tony, My Best Friend

Kelly thought it would be best if I waited to see Ted until he got out of the hospital. He had only been out of the hospital for a little while when I flew in from Texas for the day; it's only a two-hour flight to Chicago. Kelly and Ted picked me up from the airport. She drove, of course.

We went out to a restaurant, and I noticed he had a limp. He couldn't talk too much, but he pointed to a drink on the menu. Goose Island IPA. When Ted and I used to go out, he always ordered the local beer. Some things never changed. However, I think he only had about two sips of his beer that day. That determined glint had been in his eyes when he pointed to the menu, and I ordered the beer for him. It was a look that said, "I will have this. I will not let this stroke get the best of me."

We stayed out for a while and communicated as best we could. It's safe to say, I did most of the talking. But he was there. He was healthy. And he listened intensively.

He was still Ted, though. His determination was in place.

The PFO Incident

One of the reasons why I had the stroke—unbeknownst to me—was that I had a patent foramen ovale (PFO). This is a birth defect that results in a hole in the heart; it simply didn't close the way that it should have. This PFO allowed the blood clot to travel directly to the brain, rather than having it diverted to the lungs. Upon reaching the brain, the clot caused an ischemic stroke, a blockage of oxygen-rich blood to the brain. Later on—four or five months after the stroke—I was rolled into the operating room so the doctors could surgically close the PFO. Though it is recognized as a defect, having the PFO may have saved my life. Had the blood clot been sent to my lungs instead, it could have resulted in a pulmonary embolism, causing sudden death.

". . . just a localized numbing agent. It is a routine procedure," I heard the doctor saying to Kelly. "He'll be awake, but he won't feel a thing. We'll apply a medical device to close the PFO. We can do the whole procedure with a catheter tube so he will have no visible scarring, and there will be a short recovery period."

Those words were likely a comfort to Kelly. After all, we were already in the midst of a very long-term recovery process.

Unfortunately, things didn't go exactly as planned.

"Mrs. Baxter?" One of the doctors approached her shortly after the procedure was underway.

"Yes! Where is Ted? They said this would only take a few minutes?" she asked.

I hate the thought that she was scared for me again, but she said the doctors came to talk to her as soon as they could. Inserting the device was not as easy as they had hoped. The first time they went in, the device was too small; the second time, it was too large.

"I apologize that we weren't able to get to you sooner. The second attempt was unsuccessful as well, but the PFO is now plugged and Ted is doing well."

That second device was too large, and it proved difficult to handle. It released itself from the catheter the doctors used to guide the device into the appropriate place and started to float toward my aorta.

I saw what the surgeon was doing on the monitor, but since I couldn't talk, all I could do was think, *Holy shit! I hope he gets it the next time!*

"The device did detach from the catheter for a minute, but we were able to retrieve it quickly. No damage was done, so the recovery should be quick. We'll bring you in to see your husband very soon," the doctor told Kelly.

They were right, the recovery from the surgery was easy and uneventful, but I was far from being done with my recovery. I didn't know then that coming back from a stroke would be a lifelong journey. It was nice to be home again, but it put a new level of pressure on Kelly, who had to drive me to RIC Northbrook, which was forty-five minutes each way, for the next two and a half months—Monday through Friday.

"You've made excellent progress," the therapists at RIC would tell me, and it was true. It had been about five months since the stroke, and I was back to 70 percent of what my physical state and abilities had been before the stroke, but that wasn't good enough for me. I pictured it like a barometer: My body before the stroke was the goal. I wanted to, ultimately, get as close as I could to that pre-stroke physical state, so I had to push myself back up to that mark.

Start with a Plan

Kelly knew my frustration.

The physical growth was coming along, that was true.

"The RIC therapists are happy with your progress, Ted. You are doing great," she told me one afternoon.

But I wanted to talk. I wanted to hold conversations.

Kelly wanted that too. We had just pulled out of the parking lot, finally heading home for the first time since the stroke.

I was happy that it meant I was one step closer to normalcy. I looked over, and Kelly was staring at the front of the RIC building. I could see her shoulders shaking before I heard her sniffles.

I fought for the words to ask why she was crying now, at such a good moment, and came up with, "What?"

"Oh, Ted. I was so worried about losing you. And then, I was so grateful to have you, to know that you were going to live. But now . . . now I'm worried about the future. What if you never speak again? Are you going to be okay? Are we going to be okay?"

I put my hand on hers. I couldn't answer her, of course, but I was confident. I was determined. I wasn't going to let her down, and I certainly wasn't going to give up. After a few minutes, she calmed down and we were moving again.

"I have an idea, Ted. I've been talking to Jeannette. She and Tom want to help. She and I think that flash cards might help you."

She pulled the car into the parking lot of a local bookstore. "Are you okay walking in?"

I was. I nodded my head yes.

"We'll just go see what they have," she said.

We walked in, and Kelly walked toward the back of the store, keeping pace with my slower gait. We reached the flash card section, walked past the SAT study cards, and past those meant for fourth, third, and second graders. We landed directly in front of the kindergarten flash cards.

"Good?" Kelly asked.

I smiled. We perused the various cards and workbooks but left with only a pack of first words flash cards. It was a good starting point, and Kelly agreed that she would come back and pick up some of the workbooks when I was ready.

But it wasn't only the words themselves. I could say a few and I could understand several others, but stringing them together was pure frustration. It took me weeks to comprehend what full sentences meant, like, "An apple a day keeps the doctor away." While this was some progress, the comprehension didn't last. I would say it, understand it, and immediately forget it. Moments later, I didn't know what I had just said. My memory was shot!

Kelly

He had a plan for how he was going to approach his therapy. Whether it was the physical or the speech therapy, he had a plan. For example, he created a home education program. We started with one-word flash cards.

"Ready?" I'd ask, the deck of cards facedown in front of me. He was always ready, so I'd flip up the card.

"B— b— b—"

"Banana," I would finish for him.

"Ba . . . na . . . na . . . na." He would get the sounds out, but they wouldn't always be in the right order or at the right pace. But he wasn't going to give up.

"Ba. Na. Na," he'd say.

And then, "Ba. Na. Ba . . . nana. Banana."

"Yes! That's it," I would say, excited.

We'd flip through several cards, half a dozen or so at a time.

"What is this, Ted?" I'd ask, when we came back to the first card again. He would look at the picture, then at me, and then at the picture. He would search for the information, but in only a few minutes' time, it had already disappeared. He shook his head. *Oh my gosh, you just had it.* I would silently cheer him. Then, I would get upset for him. Then, I would get frustrated, and I would have to walk away. But he didn't. He was determined.

There was some excitement in the work, some noticeable growth, and that made it easier to keep going.

"Look, Ted. You have a package." I sat by and watched as he opened the box that had come from Jeannette. She was trained in special education but was working as a high school principal at that time.

"Workbooks," I said as he pulled them out, not overlooking the irony of the situation. This was a man who was a mathematical, financial, problem-solving superstar, and now we were excited about kindergarten through third-grade workbooks.

He was happy to have them and the flash cards for five-, six-, and seven-year-olds. He worked on coloring books and fill-in-the-blank sentence books with problems like, "An _____ a day keeps the doctor away."

"BlackBerry," he said.

"What did you just say?"

"BlackBerry," he responded, and I stared at him, amazed. He was pointing to it and calling the device by name. It was 2005, and at that time, BlackBerries were the hot thing in mobile phones. He was one of the few people in his company who had one, and he had absolutely lived on his BlackBerry before the stroke, so maybe I shouldn't have been shocked. But I was. He couldn't say more than half a dozen words, but this one came naturally.

"BlackBerry," he said again and smiled. I handed him his Black-Berry and smiled back.

Not all words—few, in fact—came so easily. We laughed about the mistakes and the struggles as he recovered. That was the great thing: how he found humor in this craziness coming out of his mouth. Sometimes, he would just shake his head and we'd laugh. Because it's crazy. Aphasia—seeing how the brain processes speech—is a strange thing.

— — —

We did laugh about the mistakes, but there was frustration, too. I couldn't say what I wanted to say, but that didn't mean that I was any less intelligent.

"Aphasia is an impairment of language affecting the production and comprehension of speech and the ability to read or write. This is not a loss of intelligence," the therapist told me. "We know that. You know that. But a lot of people don't know that."

It was true. I had to be understanding of how others perceived me. I didn't know about this aspect of aphasia[1] before my stroke, so how could I expect others to understand? I just had to work harder to recapture my memories and comprehension. It was never fast enough, and it was frustrating to lack the ability to interact with others as I once had. Every month, I got better with practice . . . but my progress was extremely slow!

"B— b— b— beeeee," the woman on the computer screen would emphasize the sounds of the letters and the movement of the lips and tongue. One letter after another—first the vowels and then the consonants. This was the first application that I had for the computer that would teach me how to form words letter by letter.

"Beeee," I would mimic, trying so hard to form the letter perfectly with my mouth. The building blocks in these early days were small, but they were crucial.

---

1 Aphasia is a communication disorder caused by damage to the brain that impairs the ability to convey or share information and feelings, especially when speaking. It may also affect writing, reading, and comprehension of language.

I quickly found that the rehab process took different forms. The outpatient program at RIC Northbrook had many tools.

"Today, we'll try a crossword puzzle," the speech therapist would say during lunch breaks. Some probably would have scoffed at the idea of doing work during their lunch. I didn't, but that doesn't mean that I didn't struggle with it. Making sense of words, speaking them (even within my own head), spelling them . . . all of it was excruciating.

That was just lunch—the real sessions took place before or after. I had group speech therapy every day, too, and that was torture. The therapist wasn't speaking only to me but to a group of three of us. All of us had a different "flavor" of aphasia. I wasn't even sure I knew what the word *crossword* meant, and the puzzles proved extremely challenging.

"What do you think about this?" a therapist would ask. The picture could have been of anything. Some were landscapes and others were ordinary objects. It didn't really matter what it was, because at that point, some of the other patients could talk about it, but I was limited to yes, no, or all right.

Unfortunately, the group meetings with that therapist did not result in the desired rapport. Not for me. I was frustrated with the exercises and even more so with the group aspect of the therapy. It wasn't working for me, not with the particular form of aphasia I had. But at the time, I didn't have a choice.

"What do you think about this?" she'd ask about something else.

I want to rip up your therapy notebook and get out of here, I'd think, but I could only say, "All right."

Fear and Frustration

I often say that I didn't get discouraged, but that isn't entirely true. I had a bit of hidden anger and frustration.

"How was therapy?" Kelly asked.

"No," I said, shaking my head. I pointed at the briefcase beside the desk and the filing cabinet in the corner.

"I know," she said. And she did know. I wasn't alone in my frustration. "It'd be wonderful if you could do all of that again," she said.

I used to present reports. I used to give speeches at conferences, to the clients in Tokyo, staff in London, CEO in Chicago . . . I was so fluent.

"You're getting better, though, Ted. You're making improvement," she reassured me.

"Yes," I said, but only because I couldn't say no fast enough. At this point, I had been home for two months. My competencies, my work, my gift for finance were completely gone. This was not how my life was supposed to go. I was supposed to be able to get better right away and return to work. I was frustrated, angry, sad. I barely understood those feelings before my stroke—who had time for that? But by now—about five months after the stroke—I lost it all. I was on the verge of tears every night.

What if I can never talk to you again, to my family again, to anyone again? The questions turned round in my head, but I couldn't ask them aloud. Kelly knew, though.

"You'll speak again, Ted. You don't ever give up," she told me.

She was right, but there were moments when the frustration would work its way in and the fear would take hold. In that first year after my stroke, I worried about getting into conversations with friends, that they would be embarrassed by me. Maybe they wouldn't want to converse with me because they didn't have the time to sit and talk to me, to wait while I found the words. I couldn't fluently summarize my thoughts or ideas into coherent sentences until I found some of the words. Until I could speak to them, I didn't want to see my friends. *They wouldn't want to talk to me like this anyway,* I would rationalize. The truth, though, which I soon realized, was that these were my truest friends, those willing to take time to come see me. Real friends will always be patient, and as soon as I recognized that fact, it became much easier for me to participate in conversations.

"The words are there, Ted. There in your brain. They didn't go away, but they are hiding. You have to find them again," one of the therapists told me, perhaps seeing my frustration. "You just have to find the key that unlocks the door, and then you'll have them all back again."

You know what they say—there are reasons why God put you in this world. He gives you a purpose to exist. I thought I had known mine before the stroke, but that wasn't going to fit any longer. I would have to find a new purpose and life mission.

CHAPTER 7

Not Fast Enough

As the months passed, I continued to push myself as an outpatient. I set small goals and worked little by little toward getting better. I didn't know where my effort would lead, but I knew it would be an improvement. The physical therapists at RIC Northbrook seemed to understand my need to push my physical state. I was determined to build myself up, even beyond where I was before my stroke, and they did the best they could to help me without letting me hurt myself.

During lunch breaks, I went outside with one of the physical therapists. "Take a shot," I was told. I stood halfway between the foul line and the hoop itself and looked up at the basket. I closed my eyes to concentrate my effort, bent my knees slightly to give myself a little more power, and pushed the basketball upward as hard as I could. I felt it leave my fingers.

The ball traveled upward, but only for a short distance before it began its downward descent again, missing the hoop by more than two feet.

"It's getting better, Ted. Closer than yesterday. Do you want to shoot again?" the therapist asked.

Even getting the ball that far in the air had taken a tremendous amount of effort, but I took the ball and closed my eyes again.

We followed the same sequence of therapy sessions every week for four weeks, Monday through Friday. But one day that first summer after my stroke, two or three therapists organized about fifteen of us together onto a bus and took us to a gym in the nearby Jewish Community Center (JCC).

"It'll be fun," I heard one of the therapists saying to one of the patients, who was unsure about the unexpected field trip. "We'll all enjoy a change of scenery." It was true. The JCC had an auditorium where you could see speakers give presentations. It had racquetball courts. And, it had a gym—a big gym.

"A little bigger than the RIC gym?" one of the therapists remarked to me as we walked in for the first time. I was quite pleased. RIC in the city had only five or six workout stations, but this was a real gym, complete with ten treadmills and several elliptical machines. As we kept walking through the facility, I took it all in. There were more machines for lower body workouts—quads, glutes, and so on. There were pull-down machines, bench press machines, military press machines. There were so many possibilities, and I was immediately excited.

"You're free to try any of these," the therapist said after noting which machines were RIC approved for us. "I'll be right over there." And just like that, I was standing in that gym, watching the therapist pick up a cup of coffee and take a seat on the far end of the room.

I quickly became increasingly comfortable in that gym, and I watched the therapists as I walked on the treadmill. I could feel the muscles in my legs loosening and welcoming the movement. And I watched as the therapists stood with their coffees and walked toward the door, likely wanting a couple of minutes to talk among themselves in the sunshine. As soon as that door closed behind them, I started pushing the button.

My legs moved faster and faster, and then I was jogging. The treadmill was set at 5 mph, fast enough that I had to make the switch to a jogging motion. I pushed the button again and watched the speed climb to 5.2 mph, then 5.3 mph.

"What are you doing?" I heard the yell before I looked up to see the therapist rushing through the door and directly toward me. "Stop!"

I slowed the speed to a walk and then slower still, until I came to a stop. Then, I stepped off and looked at the therapist, who led me toward the same door they had just entered through. Once outside, with the door shut again, the group of therapists looked right at me.

"Ted, you can't do things like that. If you were to fall . . . you're putting yourself and the RIC program at risk. The medical care, the lawsuits. You can't take those chances, Ted. It is not acceptable."

"I . . . don't . . . care," I tried to say. Looking straight at the therapist who had reached me first, I muttered, "I . . . have to . . . run again." *I am going to run faster than I ever have before*, I promised myself.

That was the only time I ever pulled a stunt like that, though. You can imagine, I'm sure, that the next time we went to the gym at the JCC, the therapists stayed inside, sipping their coffee and keeping a close eye on me.

The Monotony of Routine

I still wasn't happy with the speech therapy I received at RIC Northbrook. We followed the same routine every week.

This included the Boston Naming Test (BNT), which assesses anomic aphasia, an impairment of the ability to name objects. The BNT uses sixty drawings of objects, some common and some less so. The purpose is to name them—banana, axe, donkey, motorcycle, and so on—to test a person's memory.

The weekly routine also included the Western Aphasia Battery (WAB), which uses thirty-two tasks in eight groups to assess language function. This information is used to determine the degree of, and the type of, aphasia.

We used the sixteen increasingly complex configurations of the

Visual Form Discrimination Test to determine if we could discrimi-
nate between different geometric shapes every week.

And we did the Wechsler Memory Scale, which tested various
memory functions—auditory, visual, and immediate memory versus
delayed memory.

This was the routine. Every week. I was growing more and more
frustrated with each repeated task, because in my eyes, I wasn't progressing, except for the finger-tapping test.

"Okay, now tap your left index finger," the therapist said. This
was the finger-tapping test, which was meant to assess the neu-
romuscular system. The concept was to do a direct comparison
between the left and right side of the body. She shook her head,
squinted her eyes, and looked at me. "You're wrong. You're tapping
your right finger."

"I know."

"No, Ted. Tap your left finger," she said when I tapped with my
right hand again.

"Really?" I asked her, and even with my limited speech, it was
clear that I was being sarcastic. I was pissed that we were finger tapping again, three weeks in a row. I was bored. My comprehension was
coming back, but the therapist was strict. She didn't let me go. She
was taking notes about what I did or didn't do. She would tell me to
clap two times, then four times. I was always thinking about the test
and measuring my progress myself rather than listening to what the
therapists were saying.

I would undergo the same evaluation every Monday, the same battery of tests every week, and still . . . I wasn't progressing.

"This isn't enough," I told Kelly when she came to pick me up one
day. The therapists were too concerned with following the textbook
process, and that wasn't enough for me. I wanted to move, I wanted
to grow faster, and I needed a variety of activities.

Kelly understood and was willing to help, though I came to realize
later that the repetition had a purpose. While it felt repetitive to me,
the clinicians were trying to give me the time and space that I needed

to develop my speech. They would move around the room, for instance, asking questions of everyone in the group, and if a patient got stuck on an exercise, then they would simply move on and come back to that problem two or three sessions later. But I couldn't get past my frustration. In my mind, at that time, I wasn't getting any better or moving forward, and it was because I was being subjected to the same tests over and over again.

I needed spontaneous, casual conversation added to these exercises.

From Northbrook to the City

Kelly had to be my advocate, because I wasn't ready to speak for myself yet, especially through the phone.

"Do you have an outpatient speech therapy program?" she asked and stood listening for quite some time. "Wow! Yes, that would be wonderful." She paused to listen again. "Yes, we can do that . . . Great! Yes. We'll see you then."

It was that phone call that connected me with therapist Melissa Purvis at the main RIC facility in Chicago. This had to be in addition to the therapy that I was already doing at RIC Northbrook, which meant leaving one to drive directly to the other two times per week, but it was entirely worthwhile. Melissa was a great speech therapist.

"What's wrong, Ted?" Kelly asked one night on our drive home from the Chicago facility.

"Tired," I replied.

"It's a lot—to be driving back and forth. Do you want to keep doing it?" I could hear the hope in her voice. I know that it must have been torture for her, always carting me around while trying to keep up with her undergrad classes and fielding many telephone calls from family, friends, and others who were concerned with my recovery. Kelly was also researching the various aphasia programs all over the country, to determine the best one for me.

"No."

"You want to cancel your sessions with Melissa?" she asked.

"No," I answered as she pulled up to a red light. She turned and then asked me again, like she was making sense of my response.

"You want to leave Northbrook?"

"Yes," I said.

So after that, we sold the house in Kenilworth in order to move into the city, on Erie and Rush. The new place had a lot of light and great views, but even better was the fact that I'd be close enough to walk the five or six blocks to the RIC facility. That meant that I could continue seeing Melissa and enroll in RIC's physical therapy department. And it gave Kelly a well-deserved break.

Kelly

When the real estate agent came and put the sign up, Ted said, "What's that?"

I said, "Remember, we had that conversation ... ?"

It wasn't that he didn't remember us talking about selling the house. He didn't comprehend it.

"We're going to sell the house because right now you're not working, and the rehab's going to take a long time, and it's in the city, so until you're back to working ...

"When you go back to work, then we can reassess where we want to move, but for now, I don't want the stress of this house payment."

"No," he'd say, shaking his head and waving hands. I knew what he meant. "Oh no, no. I'm going to go back to work soon."

But I knew that wasn't going to happen.

— — —

We moved at the end of August, about eight months after my stroke. Moving was laborious: going back and forth, back and forth, every couple of days for about two weeks. That time is a little blurry. We hired a moving company to move all the furniture, and we put some of our belongings in storage. Kelly had to figure out what should go in storage, and when we arrived at the storage place, she told me what to do.

"Ted, just pick up these four boxes and set them on that table," she said, pointing at them to emphasize. She had to lay out the instructions basically and clearly so I could understand. This is how it had to be.

Despite the frustrations of moving, it was worthwhile. Living in the townhouse was better for me because it was in the heart of Chicago. I had everything in front of me, and I didn't have to drive. I couldn't drive, so being able to walk everywhere was wonderful. There were a couple of delis I passed on my way home from RIC where I could have lunch. I also had direct access to large gyms, larger even than the one at JCC. I joined a couple of them, including Crunch Fitness. I had real freedom again, in day-to-day life and also at the gym. That helped my post-stroke life both physically and mentally. From a rehab perspective, all this exercise helped my physical recovery, my comprehension, and my speech, but it also helped my mental state. I felt more independent and more in control. I felt more like myself.

I timed my entrance into Crunch Fitness because I didn't want to have to try to explain my intentions in front of a lot of people, so I would wait until late in the evening to go. By that time, most people had gone home to settle in for the night. There were a couple of machines in use, but the facility was much more manageable and less populated at this time of the day.

When the manager approached me one night shortly after I joined the gym, I smiled. I knew going in that it wouldn't be easy, but I started a conversation with him. I needed to tell him what I needed from the gym. It was difficult to explain, with a limited vocabulary, but eventually he understood. I had to be paired with a good trainer who would be patient with my recovery process—someone who could reteach me how to do certain exercises. The manager had the perfect trainer in mind.

The next time I entered the gym, I was introduced to an ex–San

Diego Chargers running back. I learned a lot from our sessions, but the lesson that really stuck with me was the concept of muscle memory. He talked about it often. I had to perform the same exercises every time I came in, until finally, they stuck. I would repeat these exercises enough that I would eventually be able to perform them without conscious effort. I had to rediscover my muscle memories.

— — —

"Good evening," our neighbor would say as I stepped off the elevator of our apartment building in the evening.

"Is there anything I can help you with?" the gym employees would ask when I came in each day.

"What can I get for you?" I'd be asked at the deli.

In the city, there was no way I could avoid the people who lived in our building, in the streets during my walk to RIC, or in the various businesses I patronized—Starbucks, restaurants, the gym. I was immersed. It was a big city and, at times, overwhelming. I was surrounded by people conversing, so I needed to learn to do so as well. I had to figure out how to answer them, and that was a tough job. In the meantime, I found ways to avoid conversation and took advantage of those quiet, relaxing moments.

I often went on walks by myself at six thirty in the morning, when the sun wasn't up yet. Of course, there were street lamps in Chicago, so I could see well enough, but no one was out walking that early in the morning but me, so I'd have some alone time. It gave me the opportunity to speak to just myself, in my own head, and I understood exactly what I wanted to say. Conversation aloud, with others, wasn't possible at that point. I still had so far to go in the recovery process.

Kelly

It was hard. But then, he slowly started to show his independence again. I caught him running on the treadmill in our townhome one day. I said, "Hey, you can't run on the treadmill!"

He shooed me away with his hand, so I said, "If you're going to run on the treadmill, you have to put the little leash on so if you fall, it shuts off."

And he said, "Fuck that." I remember that so clearly: "Fuck that."

After maybe eight months, he didn't want me to go with him to his doctor's appointments. Because he was able to do it, he wanted to do it by himself. He'd figure out what the doctor said we needed to do, and I knew if I had questions, I could call the doctor myself. So I let him go to the appointments by himself.

That was the good thing about moving downtown. He couldn't drive early on, but he could walk to Starbucks. Of course, they looked at him like he had twelve heads because he couldn't say what he wanted. Sometimes, he'd write it down on a piece of paper before he left our apartment and then point to it when he got there.

"Yeah, it says a tall latte," I'd say. Then, he'd show the paper to the guy at Starbucks. But he was never embarrassed to try to talk. He was never embarrassed.

Adjusting to Aphasia

Acceptance. They say it is a phase of recovery, a phase of dealing with loss. And I was contending with a loss of sorts. I had to recognize what had happened, what it meant, and how bad it was. I had to accept that it was not going to completely go away. Before I could make progress with my recovery, there had to be acceptance. I had to recognize that I had aphasia, and I couldn't simply make it go away. In time, I might be able to lessen the effects by following a rehab plan, but it would always be there in some form.

The words were no longer there. It's like someone deleted my databanks. It took me through the summer and into the fall to accept that. Then, I had to figure out what to do that could make the aphasia less blatant when I had conversations with people. My hope was that I wouldn't have to worry about being able to talk to people after two or three years of working hard to fix my speech. It was a problem, a set of parameters I needed to deal with. It might take me some time, but I was young and resilient, and I knew how to conquer problems. I understood physical therapy and working out and rebuilding strength. I could do all that. But, speech . . . that was a totally different concept. I didn't know how to get mine back. It required mental adaptation and a lot of practice.

Those early weeks and months after the stroke, part of my mind honestly believed I could push my brain to a reasonably quick recovery, in the same way I was powering forward to recapture my body. I was using my anger, determination, and natural drive all the way through RIC Northbrook to bring the right side of my body back to life, to get rid of my limp, and to regain my physical strength. I privately assured myself that my speech would follow the same course.

"You have aphasia, Ted," Melissa, my therapist at the time, essentially a jack-of-all-trades, would reiterate quite often. She knew that I wasn't happy with the rate of improvement.

I have a window . . . a small time frame. I have to make progress, fast. Time is ticking . . . I need to get back to my job, I thought. She didn't understand.

"You have to face what you have been dealt," she'd say, as if reading my thoughts. I didn't want to accept that there was a chance that the state I was in—the aphasia—was permanent. I wasn't ready to accept it yet, and without acceptance, the recovery I sought was out of my reach.

There wasn't one tried-and-true route back to full, unimpeded speech. And not having a way out, a way through, forced me to face what I tried so hard not to. This was permanent. This wasn't just my present but my future as well.

This was my lowest point. Not during the stroke and not right after when everyone and everything was a blur I couldn't decipher. This moment when I realized the aphasia was perpetual was the one that dragged me down, deep into the darkest parts of myself. It took longer still to accept that my previous life, my job at Citadel, was no longer in my future.

Acceptance was something I put off as long as I could until I felt my recovery was hitting a wall.

Acceptance was what happened when I realized that wall was me.

The Book Club I Didn't Join

The director of the aphasia department at RIC in Chicago is Leora Cherney. She and I had a conversation about my speech progression not too long after I realized my aphasia was stubborn and continuous.

"Our department does offer a few options beyond the usual therapies, if that is something you would be interested in," she said. She had my attention. "We host a weekly aphasia club, which has a wide range of activities that are meant to be fun but will also help you regain your speech. That club meets in the morning, and then after the lunch break, many come back for the book club designed for people with aphasia."

She hadn't even finished describing the clubs before I had put up a figurative wall. I didn't want to join the aphasia club or the book club.

"You might want to consider the club, Ted," said Barry Schaye, an older man who'd had a stroke five or six months before me. I met him through Kelly, who was introduced to him by his wife. Kelly met Barry's wife at one of the stroke caregiver sessions that was offered by RIC. He became a good friend of mine, though the effects of his stroke were completely different from mine. While he found words and sentences much easier than I did, his speaking was slow. But when I listened to his sentences and words, they sounded perfect. He had a limp on his right side, and he couldn't move his right leg and arm. He taught me what to expect in my life as a person with aphasia. He was more experienced than I was, and he was able to explain how his life had changed.

"The people who meet at the book club are just like you and me. They will make you feel welcomed," he said, but I didn't want to hear that. Joining a book club was just going to get in the way of my recovery. I had steps to take to reach my goals, and I didn't see how joining a club and sharing recovery time with others was going to help me recover faster. I needed one-on-one involvement. At least, that's what I convinced myself.

He quickly let the subject drop for the moment. "Let's go get some coffee," he offered, and we did. Barry and I started routinely getting coffee each day. After that, we started going to the movies each week and out to dinner often. We explored other things that the city had to offer, too. It was nice to have someone who understood where I was in my recovery and in life. Barry was the first person I truly let in, and I knew, even then, that he was good for me, and he soon became a great friend. I always bounced my ideas and comments off him to get an honest perspective. This was a person who had experienced a stroke, like I had. Every so often, though, he would return to the topic of the aphasia clubs. "You should come to our book club. It's a great place to practice your speech. Or, you can just listen to the teacher and what others have to say about the books."

I didn't listen to that advice. *I don't need that now. I can do this on my own, at my own pace. I won't have time for that. I'll be better soon and back to work*, I thought.

I saw my recovery as another exercise, another project to accomplish, like passing the CPA exam, earning an MBA from Wharton, or studying for and passing the Series 27 regulatory test for finance officers in the securities industry. If I stayed on track, I would beat it. After all, isn't that what I'd been doing my entire life? *Work hard. Be the best I can be. Climb the ladder. Get to the top.* I started that ascent in elementary school. But as time passed, I realized having a stroke and recovering from aphasia was far more than a single course.

— — —

As I started to realize that I couldn't tackle recovery in the same way that I had tackled various hurdles in my career, I started to seek advice on where I should go next to push my recovery along.

"What do you do with your days, Ted?" Melissa asked me at one of our sessions. She was a wonderful therapist and divided her attention between adults and kids with many different types of speech-related conditions.

I said as much as I could, searching my brain, working out words like *deli*, *gym*, *therapy*, and others. As we spoke, in this and other sessions, it became clear to both of us that I needed more help, different help, especially with conventional language, so I could begin to have real conversations. She gave me the number for Doreen Kelly Izaguirre, a private speech therapist.

But Melissa wasn't the only one who had ideas regarding what I should do next. I knew that Kelly had been doing a lot of research, so I asked Kelly what she recommended. She had another option for me—one that I would not have expected.

"We're going to make a trip to Michigan," she responded.

PART 2

-

Early Life

CHAPTER 8

Relentless Since Birth

had the drive to be the best quite early in life, even in elementary school.

I was born November 17, 1963, the fifth of five boys. The only sibling younger than me was my sister, Nancy. It went Tom, Gary, Jeff, Scott, me, and then Nancy. Tom is eleven years older than me; Nancy is four years younger. I shared a room upstairs with Scott, and my three oldest brothers shared one downstairs. We lived with our parents and our maternal grandmother in an average-sized house in Valley Stream, a small town on Long Island, New York.

We were a close-knit family. My mother and father were all about us kids. Whenever they took a vacation, it was with all of us. I remember all eight of us in my Dad's station wagon, driving across the country to see relatives. I was just an eight-year-old kid, but I sat in the front seat, reading the maps and figuring out how to get from Long Island to Missouri, where my aunt, uncle, and cousins lived.

One night, when we all went to a restaurant for dinner, the waitress gave me a kids' menu. But I wanted the fish filets on the regular menu. The kids' menu had cartoon food, stuff like burgers and hot dogs named after clowns.

I moped, and my brothers started to laugh at me.

My mother was sitting next to me and scowled at my brothers before turning to me. "What's the matter?" she asked.

"I don't want the kid food," I answered, pushing the folded paper menu away from me. I got the fish filets that night.

Our family was also bound by our love of sports. From my early childhood on, I was a jock. Our whole family played a lot of sports. That love of athletics further fueled my desire to be the best.

From a Psychology Report That My Brother Tom Wrote in College

The center of Ted's life is sports. It is here where Ted is going to succeed or fail in life. All aspects of his life are touched by it. Eating habits are affected because everyone in the family eats at different times, since no one is ever home at dinner time because of practice. Or else someone must eat early because he's going to practice that night. Even awakening in the morning is different. On a typical Saturday morning, Tom will go out at eight o'clock to baseball practice, while Gary and Jeff go out at nine o'clock to practice. Scott will have his practice at ten o'clock, and Ted's practice is at twelve o'clock. Dad will probably make two trips to take Gary, Jeff, and Scott to practice, while Mom takes Ted to his practice. Nothing in this family is done by routine, and everything is centered around sports. In many cases, this unorthodox method of routine might inhibit a family's relationships, but in this case, it strengthens them.

All four of Ted's older brothers are or were outstanding in athletics in high school. They stood out in baseball, football, and basketball. Ted was part of this because he always attended these events . . .

At this point in Ted's life [nine years old], he has not reached full physiological development and cannot use his small muscles to his fullest advantage . . . I think he is being inspired by his need and desire to be as good as his older brothers . . . I feel he tries to compensate [for this lack of skill at this point in his life] in two ways:

1. Ted reads and studies sports to such a degree that he can talk about sports on the same level as any one of his brothers. He doesn't do this only because he feels he has to but because he too loves sports.

2. Ted has a great imagination and sometimes tells tall stories . . . I don't think this is bad, because he is trying to make an impression and follow in the footsteps of his brother [Tom]. I think it is a good sign because it shows Ted has the imagination to be thinking all the time.

Finding Focus in Finance

I was inspired, not just to do well on the field or court. I wanted to be the best in the classroom as well. There were good reasons for me to strive for that. For one, I knew my father was paying for my three older brothers to go to college, but he wouldn't be able to pay for Scott or me to go to college. I also knew that getting As in my high school courses would give me more opportunities to select and go to a better university that suited my needs. Eventually, getting a better college education equates with a great job and a great company. I also had an accident when I played football in eighth grade that shifted my focus.

I was playing quarterback in football, and one night while we were practicing, I took the football, faded back, and threw a pass—but there was an offensive lineman blocking the defensive lineman, and he backed up so far that he was right next to me. My right index finger went through his helmet, scraping his face mask. My finger was so badly broken that the laceration affected the skin and the bone. This was the first time I had to make a big decision. I could try to play quarterback when my finger healed, or I could still play basketball and baseball and let football go. I was on the small side for football anyway. Plus, I knew academics were going to be important in my life. Between my throwing injury and my size, I could see it was time to stop playing football. I redirected my energies toward base-ball and basketball instead, while focusing on my academic success.

This was a small decision regarding my pastime, but it affected my life greatly, and it influenced the way I made bigger decisions later in life. After my stroke, I redirected my energies away from my profes-sional aspirations to focus on my recovery. I was determined to do so, because I didn't want to recover partially. I wanted to get as close to 100 percent as possible.

I also stopped playing trumpet around the time I stopped playing football. I had been using Gary's hand-me-down trumpet to play in the school band and orchestra, as well as in an extracurricular jazz band. Scott and Jeff played instruments too; I guess playing music was some-thing my parents thought was a good thing for us kids to do.

"I don't want to play an instrument anymore," I told my parents one day when I was in eighth grade.

They looked at me for a few moments, like they were shocked by the statement. "Why is that?" my father finally asked.

"I don't like it anymore. I'd rather replace music with accounting classes." The accounting class I wanted to take was held during the same period that I'd been going to band practice. "Besides, you'd know already if I was going to be a brilliant trumpet player. If I was, I would be applying to the Juilliard School. Then, I would be taking a different route."

I'm sure my parents were taken aback by the statement. I was young, but I knew already what I wanted. I loved math, and I loved working with numbers. Also, my older brother Jeff had taken accounting in college, and it seemed interesting to me. Jeff had a job taking care of financial matters for his friend. He showed me his col-lege textbooks and told me what he was doing. I thought it all looked pretty cool, the complexity of numbers, so I made it my objective to master accountancy right then, in high school. It gave me a purpose. I always liked having a purpose.

My family said I was always very serious. I thought of it as being determined. I always had that drive within me, all the way back to when I was a little kid. When I was very young, I didn't know the difference between fractions and decimals. Even before the school wanted me to know such things, I was frustrated that I didn't know. My mother was patient with me.

"Don't worry, this will come—but you have to practice it every day. I'll teach you this," she said. That was good enough for me, so I practiced it every day after school. I wanted to learn a lot of things immediately. She wasn't willing to do that with every subject, though.

"It'll come," she'd say when I got frustrated with something. "You can do this, but it's not going to be right now."

I guess it stuck in my brain that I could do anything if I was motivated and determined enough. I never thought *I can't* or *I shouldn't*. Determination means you're going to do it. It meant avoiding statements like "I can't do that." Those words weren't part of my equation.

My favorite athlete, the famous role model in my life, was Magic Johnson. But he wasn't the only one I emulated. I had older brothers who were all-star athletes and set a bar I had to get over. Sports, particularly basketball and baseball, had a pretty big effect on my life. My goal was to make all-county and all-league for basketball and for baseball, and I achieved that in my junior and senior years of high school.

The sports, though, had to take a backseat to schooling. My high school offered advanced placement courses, which allowed you to earn credits that you could transfer into college. I took them all through my tenth-, eleventh-, and twelfth-grade years. I studied hard, as if I were taking the actual college course, then I took the test. I took all the classes—biology, chemistry, history, trigonometry, precalculus, calculus, and so on—and passed all the math tests with a 4 or 5 out of 5. I passed the rest with 3s or 4s. All in all, I earned thirty AP credits, a full year's worth of classes, before I had even decided which college I would attend!

One night, as I was finishing my homework when I was in the third grade, my mother told me that if you want to be the best student in school, you have to practice a lot, research, and ask a lot of questions.

Without saying it outright, she was letting me know how to achieve my goals to become an overachieving student and in life as a leader. And that advice stuck with me. Just like what I had to overcome when I had a massive stroke. Because of my experiences early in life, I had the tenacity to deal with the challenges presented with my stroke and aphasia. I know that if my mother were alive, she, too, would be my cheerleader and provide me support and encouragement.

CHAPTER 9

Pedal to the Metal

After I graduated high school, I decided to go to Hofstra University, a private college on Long Island known for its public accountancy program.

"It's a great school, Ted, and it will allow you to live at home. The scholarships will help," my father said to me after going with me to speak to a counselor at Hofstra. I had earned three scholarships from Valley Stream South High School. They wouldn't go far toward the tuition, but every bit helped. "You'll only have to cover tuition and books. We'll help you apply for a student loan, but you are going to want to get a part-time job," he said and then smiled at me. "You'll be fine."

I bought a used Camaro and planned to do more than just cover my necessities. I majored in financial accountancy and took computer science classes as a possible minor. I also got a full-time job at the Dime Savings Bank of New York at the bank's computerized processing facility, which handled all their bank systems across all their branches. Eventually, I was promoted to supervisor of the second shift, which meant that I worked full time while going to college as a full-time student.

I commuted to my morning classes at Hofstra University and then worked from three p.m. to eleven p.m. at the Dime Savings Bank's computer facility. I was the second-shift manager. I didn't play any sports at Hofstra, but I did organize and manage a Sunday night softball team each summer for three years. That was the only time I was with all my friends.

Hofstra was big compared to other schools on Long Island, with a student population of fifteen thousand. There was one professor I picked for every accounting class that he taught—accounting 1 and 2 and financial accounting. What I admired most about him was that he was extremely smart, especially about numbers and scheduling. He was happy to talk about his job, and I was surprised, at first, to learn that teaching wasn't all that he did. He was also a partner for an accounting firm.

"I go to work at my other job at three p.m. on Monday, Wednesday, and Friday. Tuesday and Thursday are full days. I can teach here Monday, Wednesday, and Friday from eight a.m. to one p.m., and I love to teach."

"Is it true that you develop all of the tests?" I asked as the rest of the class filed in before one of our classes.

"It's true," he said with a smile. He'd stay after class to correct those same tests and to answer questions. I often spoke to him about balancing two jobs. I wanted to emulate his time management to help me with my working and taking classes at the same time.

Like most universities, Hofstra had two sessions: fall and spring with a break between. I always took a course during that six-week winter intersession. But, my senior year, I participated in an internship program for the six-week winter intersession. In order to do so, I had to interview with ten firms—the Big Eight and two medium-sized firms.

"... all of the Big Eight accounting firms," I boasted to my mother, "and both of the others. They each offered me an internship," I added, knowing that she would be proud.

"Which will you choose? Will you be guaranteed a job after school?" she asked.

"There's no guarantee, but I have a definite chance," I told her. "I'm going with Price Waterhouse."

I knew there wouldn't be enough time to do everything—classes, internship, and my second-shift job, so I told my boss, "I need a break."

"I understand, Ted. You are certainly welcome back after the internship."

So, I took a leave of absence from the Dime Savings Bank for my six-week stint at Price Waterhouse. Then, I went back to my job and my last semester of classes.

I earned my bachelor of business administration (BBA) in three years and graduated magna cum laude and Phi Beta Kappa. It was time to leave the Dime Savings Bank for good.

"I got the job, Mom!" I happily called her to tell her that I had been offered a position by each of the ten accounting firms, and she cheered with joy. I knew that I was on the right path.

"The same place as the internship?" she asked.

"Yeah, Mom. The same place. I'm going full time at Price Waterhouse in August."

That November, after taking a fast-prep class, I took and passed all four Certified Public Accountant (CPA) sections in one shot. It meant sitting through these tests and concentrating on them for three and a half days straight.

Price Waterhouse

I was twenty years old in 1983 and working as an auditor with some of the biggest industries in New York, including Chase Manhattan, Chemical Bank, and several of the big players in the securities industry. I even branched into manufacturing and nonprofit companies. I got a taste of every industry so I could see what was most interesting to me. I decided I liked financial services.

"How's work, Ted?" my brother Tom asked me one day a few months after I'd been working at Price Waterhouse full time. I quickly learned that many people weren't as ambitious as I was, but I think my family understood.

"I applied for a position in the management consulting department," I told him.

"Wow! You're so young. Do you think you'll get it?"

"It's not easy to get into. They'll only take thirty people, from Price Waterhouse or from university masters' programs . . ."

"But, do you think that you'll get it?" he asked again.

"Yes, I do," I answered and laughed a little. He laughed with me but offered his best wishes. I got the job. I started in that department in 1985.

Those of us who were chosen were sent to study system programming at Montclair State in New Jersey for six weeks. Then, we were all sent to Tampa, Florida, for the rest of the year to build and implement a new system from scratch—from requirements definition to user acceptance to production cutover. After that, I went back to my New York office as a Price Waterhouse management consultant.

My first client was Chase Manhattan Bank, which had eight or nine locations in New York City. When you work as a management consultant, your time and billing per hour relate to the client's deadline; for example, having their financial strategy outlined and their systems and processes defined and implemented in a client-driven time frame—all of them had to be there by a specific time, complete and finished. I'd spend four days out of the week at Chase Manhattan's facilities on Wall Street and then go into the Price Waterhouse office on the fifth day. My job encompassed a wide variety of services. One month, I was working with a partner to define a model CFO for the World Bank in Washington, DC, and the next, I was working on a feasibility trade system for Lehman Brothers with a group of consultants. Then the next month, I'd evaluate the processes and systems and write user procedures of the American Stock Exchange and work on a proposal for Salomon Brothers. These were all jobs I'd been trained to do, but I had to be flexible and spontaneous because I never knew what I'd be doing next for my client. Over the next few years, I took on Smith Barney and Salomon Brothers, in addition to Chase.

In 1990, when I was twenty-seven years old, I was living in a New Jersey condo I'd bought with my best friend, Tony, and commuting to New York every day. I decided it was time to take a seriously frivolous vacation, so my friend Dan and I booked an all-inclusive package—hotel, meals, all the extras—in Jamaica.

Kelly Comes into My Life

That's where I met Kelly. She had come to Jamaica for the same all-inclusive package.

"She's pretty, huh?" Dan asked, nudging me in the ribs. I swatted his arm away, fought the blush that threatened to give me away, and continued to steal glances at her. She wore her hair long, to her shoulders, and more than once, she caught me looking at her. She'd whip that hair to the side and look right back, allowing a smile to fill her face.

I could see at first glance that she was pretty, outgoing, and genuine.

"So, Kelly," I started, after breaking the ice and learning her name, "are you going to take the bus trip today?" I knew there was an activity scheduled for the afternoon, which was included as part of the all-inclusive package.

"Um . . ." She smiled and blushed. "I think so. Are you?" If she was, of course I planned to. So, we spent the day together. She had a great personality, and she was straight with me from the start—no games.

"Where are you from?" I asked her.

"I was born and raised in a very small town in Illinois," she replied.

"But you don't live there now?" I asked as we sat beside the pool.

"No, I'm living in El Toro, California, now."

"What do you do in El Toro?" I asked.

"For work?" She looked at me out of the corner of her eyes while taking a sip from one of those drinks with the little umbrella.

"Yeah, for work," I answered with a laugh.

"I'm an administrative assistant at Century 21. It's a real estate company."

We liked each other immediately.

We liked the same movies, the same music, the same food, and we both liked to travel. We hung out at the beach every day and went out every night while we were in Jamaica. When I got home from that trip, all I could think about was how I could see her again.

We started trading weekends. I'd go to California to see her one weekend, and then she'd come to the East Coast to see me the next.

We went on like this for several months, and then I decided that it was time to have a conversation about the situation. I knew I wouldn't be able to keep up the same schedule for long, because I had big plans regarding my profession. "I like you, Kelly," I told her.

"I like you too, Ted," she said with a laugh.

I smiled, but then I took on a serious tone. "Look, if we're going to do this, I want you to move to New Jersey. I'm sorry. I can't give up my job, my career at Price Waterhouse. I've been in two long-distance relationships. Neither of them worked."

"I know that," she said, and she was quiet for minute.

"Maybe you can go to school, if you want . . ."

"It's okay, Ted. I knew that I'd have to move to you. You can't give up your job, and Century 21 . . . it's a good job, but it was only meant to be a stepping-stone. It's time to figure out what I want to do. I'll move to New Jersey."

Working and Wharton

"I'm going to go back to school," I told Kelly one night over dinner. She was living in New Jersey, and we had fallen in love. Our relationship had a nice rhythm, and we were both happy.

"Really? That's exciting. Can you do that while working this job? You're quite busy as is," she said.

"It won't be easy, but I can do it."

She smiled at me. "I know you can. If anyone can, it's you."

She was being so supportive. I knew that this was someone that was going to be very important in my life. Shortly after that conversation, we decided to get married. We got busy planning, because we wanted to be wed before I started at Wharton. We were married on Long Island and then enjoyed a beautiful honeymoon at Saint John and Saint Thomas in the Caribbean. It was a wonderful calm before the chaos began.

After the wedding, it was time to get back to work. By then, I was a senior manager, and I discussed the executive MBA process with my boss, Mike Balk. Mike helped me with the necessary recommendations so I got accepted to Wharton's Executive MBA program. That meant that for the first two years of our marriage I was at class every other weekend and busy all week with work. I was still working full time with all my usual clients, while taking classes and managing homework. This is when I most appreciated the before-class lessons about time management from my previous professor from Hofstra University.

It was a hectic time in my life but a happy one, because I had someone by my side.

Kelly

There were times in the early days when it was hard because Ted was always working and going to school. He had to take the GMAT to get into grad school, and for him, that meant studying for it and taking the prep classes for the GMAT. He really dug into it. He was like that with everything. He's a preparer, for sure. He wouldn't even go to the pool with me when we were on vacation. That was hard.

"Gosh, would you just stop studying for ten minutes?" I asked him one day.

"No, I can't," he'd mutter with his face in one book or another.

On the other hand, he was also very good at helping me when I got overwhelmed. I'd tell him, "I have forty things on my to-do list."

"That's okay. Take the top three. Write those down. Do those today and forget the rest of the list." He was good at simplifying and not putting his stuff on me.

He was so focused, so organized and calm. He always had a purpose and a goal; he was always moving forward, and he was always calm about it all. Even with all that he had going on, even with his intensity, he was calm. He doesn't do unnecessary stuff. If he asked you to do something, there was a reason for it. He never started projects that he didn't finish, and he never started projects that weren't meant to benefit either his career or our life together.

And he had ways to play. Even though he was so determined, he certainly knew how to have a good time. He picked great vacation spots, romantic getaways, and restaurants, and he loved going to plays and music concerts and hanging out with our friends. Ted put 110 percent into everything he did.

CHAPTER 10

Moving, Moving, Moving: Out, Up, Everywhere

Price Waterhouse had three divisions: audit, tax, and management consulting. Each division focused on financial services. This creates a matrix in the organization of Price Waterhouse. I worked as a management consultant in the financial services industry area. By the time I earned my executive MBA, I had completed major consulting engagements for Salomon Brothers, UBS Investment Bank, Canadian Imperial Bank of Commerce, Deutsche Bank, and Chase Manhattan Bank.

And again, I was ready to tackle something new, so one day, I stopped by the office to see my boss, Juan Pujadas. He was one of my mentors, a distinguished partner who was in his midthirties at the time. He had joined Price Waterhouse at a young age and become a partner in his ninth year with the company. He made things happen and was a fantastic consultant. I made it my objective to do the same. I wanted to be in a place that would allow me to make partner quickly—at a place where I could interact with a lot of clients, use a wide array of our services, become a specialist in one or two skill sets, and manage a lot of consulting projects. It was a goal that I would eventually reach.

"What am I supposed to do next?" I asked him.

Juan said, "I'm sending you to Tokyo." I had already been to Tokyo to be involved with two potential clients and to submit proposals on two projects. In the end, we lost both of them. But those proposals were doomed to failure because they were led by Price Waterhouse New York with English speakers who hadn't lived in Tokyo. At that point, we didn't realize that the Japanese companies preferred a provider that was Japanese based. This would be a different sort of approach. "If this doesn't work in one year, then we will have to reevaluate whether it makes sense for us to have financial services consulting in Tokyo. If it works, our practice will grow, prosper, and blossom in one of the major financial cities of the world."

— — —

"You're going to move to Japan?" my mother asked upon hearing the news. "You're going to live there?"

"Yes, Mom," I replied.

"How? How will you do that? Do you even speak Japanese?"

"I'm taking a class, Mom," I said somewhat defensively, but then changed my tone. "It'll be challenging. I'll have to learn Japanese, work in a new business environment, learn Japanese customs, and blend in as much as I can." I decided that I would need to pick foreign expatriates to come with me and then to hire local staff while there. I didn't express that, though. I just said, "I'll make it work."

"What about Kelly? Is she okay with this? Does she speak Japanese?"

"Yes. She's going too. She'll have to learn the language too."

"But, what about her job?" my mother asked.

"She's putting in her notice."

Kelly did have to quit her job as an executive assistant in an investment firm. She would have to learn Japanese in order to make friends, and she'd have to go to Japanese grocery stores. She'd also have to learn their customs so she could interact with people daily.

"Are you sure about this, Ted? It's an awful lot to take on."

"I'm ready, Mom. I've always been a risk taker."

She sighed, but I heard the acceptance. "That is the truth."

Price Waterhouse already had a presence in Japan but not in financial services consulting. I had to create and grow it from nothing, while learning Japanese on the job. I had taken a short Japanese-language course in New York, but it didn't really register with me. So I was nervous about my ability to communicate once I was there.

But first, Kelly and I had to find our way around the city. When we arrived in Tokyo at the airport, they told us that we'd have to take a train into the city.

"What did he say?" Kelly asked, and I could tell that her nerves were taking hold of her.

"We have to catch a train into the city," I answered, and we both looked around. There were no trains that we could see.

"Can you read the signs?"

I shook my head and finally said, "We'll have to take a taxi." So, we decided to get a cab to downtown Tokyo—which took three hours in traffic! I asked a few questions of the driver, but he didn't understand me. I could see him in the mirror, and it was perfectly clear that he wasn't comprehending anything I said. To make things worse, once we arrived, the fare was unbelievably high!

Our second night at the Westin, we decided to go to dinner at a restaurant the concierge recommended to us. We knew the place was near the hotel, so we didn't worry about getting a taxi. We took a walk.

But Tokyo streets are nothing like American streets. Here in the United States, addresses run sequentially: 2 Main Street, 4 Main Street, 6 Main Street, and so on. In Japan, the numbers run more like 865 Main Street, 16400 Main Street, 2 Main Street. I don't know why, and at the time I didn't care enough to ask. I had enough other problems on my plate.

It took us an hour to find the restaurant, though it only should have taken us fifteen minutes. I realized then that the day-to-day in Japan would be like this. Simple things like getting to work, navigating grocery stores, reading the subway maps, and hailing taxis after a late night of work became major challenges.

"How are we going to do this, Ted?" Kelly asked.

I didn't know how to answer. The truth was there would be much bigger problems for me to solve. I had the support of Price Waterhouse. She was, more or less, on her own, though.

One Year to Profit

The Price Waterhouse Tokyo CEO gave me one year to develop a cost-effective profit and loss (P&L) performance. That meant I had to staff my practice with quality people, but I also had to bring in billable clients and execute their services. Eventually, I hired expatriates who fit my needs—two Americans, one British, one Australian. Then, I had to scour the Japanese workforce to find three or four people who were Japanese, which I managed to do, but they could only speak a little English. Afterward, I hired bilingual people who acted as a bridge between those of us who only spoke English and those of us who only spoke Japanese. But, unfortunately, these talents were hard to find. It took me four months to hire two bilingual employees.

Just getting to that point was a huge hurdle. The first time I met with a Japanese client, I couldn't have a conversation. I had to have a person next to me who spoke Japanese and could translate. Finding these Japanese people who spoke English and who also had some knowledge of financial products was the equivalent of striking gold. These guys came from towns an hour away, which made hiring Japanese staff difficult.

I wanted Japanese staff who could mimic what the expats were doing. I did a project with Chase Manhattan in Tokyo and had two staff doing the work—one expat and one Japanese—so one could tag along and learn. But I wouldn't charge the client for the second staff. That's how I started to change the metrics from mostly expats to mostly Japanese.

The next major challenge would be selling services to Japanese financial firms. My bosses from New York, London, and Tokyo knew that would take more than a year to accomplish, so in the meantime, I did small jobs from "foreign" firms I knew already existed there in Tokyo: Chase Manhattan, Salomon Brothers, Morgan Stanley, and so forth.

— — —

"Did you see the price, Ted?" Kelly asked when we looked at the listing for an apartment in the expatriate community that we had in mind. "That's JPY 1 MM per month . . . nearly $10,000 per month!"

"It's pretty steep," I responded. "But the company will cover it."

"Okay," she said, looking back down, but there was hesitation in her voice. She had it rough. She was alone most of the time, and she didn't speak any Japanese, but she was always there to support me.

Kelly

I was twenty-three when we got married, and for so long, my identity was Ted. Somebody would ask, "Where did you go to college?" And I'd say, "I didn't, but Ted went to Wharton."

That's what happens in a relationship, I guess. There were times when I was his identity, like there were times when he was mine. But it was more noticeable on my end, because I wasn't the one working. I wasn't the more powerful force in the marriage. I was independent and strong—and certainly not fearful. But I was not the go-getter, not the money-maker, not the one we moved around the world for!

— — —

When I brought in the international consultants from our Price Waterhouse New York, London, or Sydney offices, I'd have them bring their wives, if we had lunch meetings scheduled, so they had a chance to start their own relationships. The wives who accompanied their working husbands couldn't work if they didn't have their own work visas, but Kelly figured out how to handle things. For one thing, we all belonged to Tokyo American Club, and she spent a good deal of time there helping Japanese women learn English, and in turn, Kelly learned many basic Japanese customs. She also met many expatriates, mainly women, who went to the Club. They could talk about everyday things like grocery shopping, going to coffee shops, and working out, in English.

Meanwhile, I was going out to Japanese financial firms to market services and to give presentations. The problem was, I only spoke English, and the audience only spoke Japanese. I filled my Power-Point slides with pictures that bridged the gap so the audience understood what I was saying. But I wasn't closing deals because I was only getting one nod. In Japanese business culture, that meant that they were understanding the message. A second nod would have meant that they were able to translate to their business language. And the coveted third nod would have meant that I made the sale. I was only getting one. And while I brought staff with me to help, none of them translated, so it was all on me.

My Look-Alike

After a year, I finally went back to the CEO from Price Waterhouse in Tokyo.

"This practice will not work if I don't have great translation skills. I need a Japanese stand-in for me. He needs to speak Japanese, live in Japan, and get along with both Japanese and international colleagues. He also needs to be a marketer, in Japanese terms, and to have the basic building blocks of the financial services industry," I said.

"Go ahead! Good luck finding him. We were lucky to find you." He advised me to bring all the information from New York that I had and to blend it with someone in Japan who could work with Japanese institutions and staff. If I could do that, it would work.

I did find my Japanese "look-alike," as the CEO called him (though we looked nothing alike). The firm had to offer an attractive salary to bring him into Price Waterhouse Financial Services Consulting.

"You've done amazing things, Ted," the Japanese CEO said to me, and I was happy to have this client under my belt, but I also knew what came next. "It's year two now, though. You know what that means."

"I've got to sign a Japanese financial institution." I had to break that wall, and it was hard that first year. My colleagues and managers didn't know how to do it either, but I figured it out with the help of my look-alike. I taught him some of the financial services terms and tactics, and he taught me how Japanese businesses work in Japan— not from the Japanese business 101 textbook, but from an experienced Japanese businessperson. It was a two-way street.

Three months later, I broke the wall. I finally landed a project with Nomura Securities, probably the biggest global securities firm based in Tokyo. It was my biggest personal achievement. That's when I knew this practice would grow. Having Nomura as a client was the foundation of having a lot of chargeable Japanese clients. Soon, I had a lot of Japanese firms who wanted to meet us, so we listened to their issues, and then we talked about our services. They wanted proposals from us. We quickly learned the term *Keiretsu*, which means a group of loosely affiliated corporations with broad power and reach like an informal business group. These firms that contacted us had ties to Nomura. Once I had signed one, the others wanted to follow suit. That was Keiretsu at its finest, which was all explained to me by my look-alike.

By then, we were in the third quarter of year two. I had this major client as well as a few small foreign clients, and by the end of the second year, I had twenty employees, six of whom were bilingual. I changed the P&L metrics of my practice, taking it from a loss position to a stable one, and eventually it became a very profitable practice.

I did presentations for prospective clients regularly. If I landed one of them, I had to organize a project team and follow up with the senior manager. I would often be onsite at the client's office to make sure he was completing the job correctly. My day ran from

eight a.m. to six thirty or seven p.m., and then frequently, I'd go out
to dinner with prospective clients. It was intense work. Sometimes,
my family didn't understand that this wasn't a short-term project;
when you're building a new practice, you have to be there and live
by their way of life.

Nancy

I never saw him. I understood it was his career. He lived in Japan
for five years ... or however many years it was. He was on such an
intense career path that I only wanted the best for him. I couldn't
believe what he was accomplishing. So I understood, but I didn't like
it. None of us had moved away from Long Island. It was only the six
of us, and we were definitely a close-knit, tight family.

- - -

During year three of my Japanese adventure, I made partner, and by
year four, I had seventy-five employees: sixty to sixty-five Japanese
and ten to fifteen expats. I was the only partner there running the
financial services consulting area in Tokyo, which meant I no longer
had time to go out and meet clients. I'd become an administrator,
working behind a desk.

On to Hong Kong

Administration was too tame for me. I needed a more challenging
game. So, I called my boss at Price Waterhouse in London, but none
of his ideas were as appealing to me as the one I was offered by a
global investment bank who wanted to lure me away.

"So, I was approached by an executive recruiter today," I mentioned to Kelly, between bites of food. I wiped my face with my nap-
kin to hide my expression. I'm not sure if I was excited or nervous or
a little of both.

"Oh yeah?" Kelly answered as she swallowed, but I could tell that it hadn't really sunk in.

"He has a fantastic opportunity for me from a major global investment bank."

That got her attention. "Really? What kind of job? Would you really leave Price Waterhouse?"

"I might. I'm not in love with the desk job, and my boss hasn't proposed anything better . . ."

"So, what's the position?" she asked.

"Asia Pacific regional head of financial control."

She took a moment to digest it. "What's the company?"

"Credit Suisse First Boston."

"Does this mean that we are moving back to the US?"

"No. We'd have to move to Hong Kong if I get the offer from CSFB," I said.

So, after I had visited Credit Suisse First Boston's (CSFB) main office in Hong Kong and interviewed with five or six people there, I had the offer. It was a perfect match for me! A leading powerhouse global investment bank offered me a prestigious position with room to move up quickly, and the vibe was fast and exciting. Kelly and I made plans to move.

- - -

"Ted, I want to do something," Kelly told me one day before our move.

"What do you mean?" I asked her, confused by the statement.

"Something. Something. I want to do . . . something. If we move to Hong Kong, I won't have a work visa."

"What do you want to do? Do you have something particular in mind?"

"I want to learn how to cook. I mean, I want to learn how to really cook, like a chef."

"Okay, so you want to go away to culinary school?" I asked her.

"Yeah, I do." She handed me a brochure for a French culinary school in Manhattan.

"You want to go back to New York City?" I asked and then looked into her eyes. "I can't go with you. I have to take this job."

"I know," she said, and it was clear that she knew exactly what it would mean—six months apart. "Are you mad?" she asked.

I thought for a second. We were accustomed to spending time apart, and as I considered it, I knew that this was a great opportunity for her. I also knew that she would be coming back to be with me in Hong Kong after the schooling ended. "No. You should go."

So, I organized and coordinated our move from Tokyo to Hong Kong, while she was in New York. That meant that I came home to an empty house in Hong Kong for six months, but it didn't matter to me because I was all about my career moving ahead. I was visiting and managing my staff overseas as well as my staff in Hong Kong. I was living only in my Hong Kong apartment for about half of the month. I traveled to a different country every other week. It was a blast for me. I was feeding on the constant adrenaline rush and loving every minute.

When I had to go back to New York, maybe two or three times a year, I'd tell my brother Tom, and he'd give the rest of the family notice.

— — —

Credit Suisse First Boston was a big change for me. I was on the other side of the coin now, with the client that firms like Price Waterhouse courted. I had been a partner of Price Waterhouse, which was smaller than CSFB. The latter employed more than eighteen thousand people. As financial controller for Asia Pacific, I had nine country financial controllers who directly reported to me, and I visited them and traveled to New Zealand, Australia, Singapore, China, Tokyo, India, Russia, the Philippines, and then back to Hong Kong over my two-year term.

When Kelly came to Hong Kong after culinary school, she didn't know anyone. We had left all our new friends behind in Tokyo, and she had to build a new circle of friends yet again.

During our stay in Asia Pacific, Kelly would set up incredible vacations for us to get away. We went to Bali twice—once with my brother Tom and his wife. We vacationed in the Philippines, Thailand, Malaysia, Sydney, and Melbourne. We went to Hawaii twelve times while we lived in Tokyo, because it was so close. It was also great to be able to take a vacation within the United States. Hawaii was a secret hideaway for us, a needed break for me. We've been to all of the Hawaiian Islands.

I didn't want to be an absentee dad, and Kelly didn't want to be a married-single mom, so we didn't try to have kids while living in Asia-Pacific. But this began to take its toll on our relationship. We grew a little bit more apart every year.

In 2001, my global boss from CSFB, Dave Fisher, called me from New York. "You've been out there in Hong Kong for us for two years now—six altogether, including Price Waterhouse Tokyo. It's enough. We want you back in the United States to be the Americas Controller, based in New York."

CHAPTER 11

I Wanted More

After six years living out of the country, three years in almost constant motion, living and working for CSFB in New York was . . . quiet. I read textbooks from regulatory agencies dealing with the Securities and Exchange Commission and the New York Stock Exchange. Boring. I didn't like staying in one place, especially in a location that always seemed to be in the middle of one political upheaval or another, as CSFB was.

"What can I do for you, Ted?" my boss asked when I came in for a one-on-one meeting.

"I don't want to sound ungrateful, but I'm just not cut out for this job. I'm not a desk job kind of guy," I told him.

He nodded in response and thought for a moment. "What are you looking for?" he asked.

"I just need . . . a bit more excitement. I liked the travel," I replied.

"All right. Give me some time, and I'll see what I can do."

He pulled the necessary strings and jumped through the requisite hoops, and several months later, I was promoted to global head of strategic change management for financial control. I was still based in New York, but since the job was global, I was able to travel. I went to London every six weeks. I had to go to Asia Pacific once every three months, which was like going home. But then, I had to fly back to Manhattan, to sit behind a desk again.

By 2004, I'd grown tired of dealing with CSFB's daily internal politics. An executive headhunter I knew was looking for a young, dynamic global financial controller who could soon be a chief financial officer (CFO). It took nine months of flying back and forth between New York and Chicago and going through many tests and interviews to land the job. It was quite a change. I left a massive global corporation to join the organization in Chicago that had only 1,500 people. But I loved the job, which was focused in an area of finance called hedge funds (i.e., alternative investments using pooled funds that use a number of different strategies to earn return for their investors). It was a dream!

Citadel Investment Group was small in terms of the number of employees, especially when compared to CSFB, but it was large in the world of hedge funds. It was also globally diverse in terms of alternative investments producing assets. It was, in that sense, a big business, worth $15 billion or more in 2005.

The firm assembled different financial products for groups of wealthy investors and served as a hedging vehicle for the banks and investment firms. As a global financial controller, I analyzed the performance of each business division. I presented this information daily to management. In addition, I was responsible for reporting the monthly firm-wide performance to the CFO and dealing with regulatory agencies. I played a large part in the financial systems that controlled the transactions after the daily trades' execution. I also improved their processing system by putting business unit control, financial control, and systems under one roof. Besides dealing with the SEC and NYSE in Chicago, I was charged with overseeing financial control activities in London, Tokyo, and Hong Kong, as well as some remote locations in Bermuda, Mauritius, and Luxembourg. I loved the travel, but the job was intense—besides the above, I made sure we met all deadlines for the on-line production, oversaw financial IT development, handled staff issues, and more. The firm's dynamic style and speed, the bustling, active vibe, and my job, which was so much more than the standard description of the role of global controller, was so exciting. It was perfect for me.

Joining Citadel meant leaving New York City. For the first several weeks, I rented a small apartment in Chicago while Kelly sold our place in New Jersey. She joined me as soon as she could, and we began house hunting. We were excited to start a new chapter in our lives.

--- --- ---

"The realtor called. We can go see the place tomorrow," Kelly told me one day after we'd been living in the small apartment in Chicago for a few weeks. Excitement laced her voice. This move had been big for me, for my career, but Kelly also saw it as a new opportunity for our future.

She handed me the listing information.

"It's big," I said, eyes undoubtedly wide. This place was huge compared to the homes we had seen in Chicago previously.

"Big enough for kids—a couple, at least," she responded with a shy smile.

I smiled back. "Tomorrow works."

We bought the house, but we never got around to having the kids.

Change on the Horizon

We both knew something had gone south in our relationship. In fact, we'd started seeing a marriage counselor a year or so earlier. Children were on the table in our discussions. So was divorce. Something wasn't working anymore. But we remained close friends (and still are).

And my legs hurt, especially my right leg. I'd talked to my doctor many times during previous years about my varicose veins. He insisted they were superficial and nothing to worry about. I'd started wearing knee-high support socks several years before. My doctor advised me to wear the ones that went all the way up onto the thigh, but since I worked out every day and the doctors weren't concerned, I wasn't concerned.

- - -

In March of 2005, I told Kelly about my plans to go to Mauritius for business.

"I have to visit Mauritius for a couple of days, for the company," I told her. I knew that it was a gorgeous locale in the middle of the Indian Ocean, two thousand miles off the African coast.

"Would you have any interest in turning the trip into a vacation?" I asked her.

She was definitely interested, so we booked reservations for a full week, excited to escape the cold Chicago weather.

Poor Kelly; this was the trip where she ended up staying in the room with the flu for most of the time. Then we went home. It was no problem for me to spend more than twenty hours flying to and from that island paradise, given how often I traveled for work.

Three weeks later, I would go from a place where life was great—sitting on a beautiful beach in Mauritius—to being in a hospital fighting for my life.

What a difference a few weeks make.

PART 3

Building a
New Path

CHAPTER 12

Turning Point

"We're going to make a trip to Michigan," Kelly said. I remember being shocked by the statement. I expressed my confusion.

"UMAP. I've done the research. The University of Michigan's aphasia program is among the best in the country," she explained.

I liked the idea of the road trip. I was able to get away and focus my mind on only one thing.

Kelly

I called UMAP in November 2005, seven months after the stroke. They said they didn't take anyone until they were at least one year post-stroke. We went up to Michigan to see the facility anyway.

Going to UMAP

Sometime in December 2005, Kelly and I took our road trip to see the UMAP facility. In addition to moving forward with my recovery, we also decided that it was time to welcome a new addition to our lives. I needed a companion, so we stopped at a breeder in Michigan and bought a pug, which turned out to be a wonderful therapeutic animal. We named the pug Sullivan, after Dr. Terence Sullivan, who was my general doctor. He had been with me since the beginning. He knew a lot of people in the city, and he always had tips or comments for me. He had a lot of patience with me after the stroke, and he listened to what I was trying to say. Patience is a virtue, and boy, I learned that quickly. He became a sort of confidant for me regarding the potential implications of the stroke and aphasia.

While Kelly had many discussions behind the scenes with the UMAP staff, I sat in on a couple of sessions with a group of people who had experienced strokes and were in the middle of their six-week program. A couple of them had come back for a second time, some as young as twenty-five and some in their fifties or sixties. They taught the rest of us a bit about what to expect from the program. I thought that this program could be a good fit and a valuable opportunity for me.

Kelly arranged for me to start at UMAP in January 2006.

So nine months after my stroke, Kelly and I packed my clothes and moved me into the Ayres Hotel in Ann Arbor, Michigan, for six weeks. It was absolutely freezing—even colder than Chicago.

Kelly

The people at UMAP strongly advise their stroke patients to stay in one of the two hotels they use; the shuttle bus drivers understand that their passengers have aphasia and really watch over them. They also advise the caretakers, like me, to go back to our own homes and leave their loved ones alone to let them be somewhat independent. So I brought Ted to Ann Arbor, got him checked in and set up with the staff, stayed at the hotel with him for a couple of days, and then drove back to Chicago.

But before I went back to Chicago, Ted and I met Joy, a fantastic speech therapist at UMAP.

- - -

Kelly and I met Joy Fried together my first day at UMAP. After we talked for a few minutes, Joy sat me down alone.

"I don't really understand what you're saying. You are jumbling your words," she said and paused to allow me to digest the information. "Your brain doesn't know how to reorder them. Part of it is a lack of words. You understand the concept, but your brain can't translate that into words—the right words in the right order." I knew it was true, and I knew it was hard, and I cried there in her office. "Don't get down on yourself, Ted. You almost died. You didn't, though, so you've conquered the first challenge. Now, let's just take it easy, work on the basics. The rest will come."

Joy was very honest and a pleasure to work with. She became my coach, and she challenged me as the program continued. If I had a bad day, she'd talk to me about it the next morning.

"What happened to you last night?" she'd ask. "I talked to one of my therapists, and she said you got very frustrated with the verbs." Joy was nice, but she didn't let things go. She was also fair and not strict.

Kelly

That first night in Ann Arbor, before I returned to Chicago, Ted and I went to dinner at Zingerman's Deli. While we ate, Ted told me, "Joy said I'm not comprehending well."

I don't think he used the word *comprehending*, though. These conversations were never easy. They took a long time.

"The girl," he said.

"You mean Joy?" I asked.

Then he nodded. Our conversations would go back and forth in that way for a while, until I eventually understood what he was trying to get across. In this instance, it was, "Joy said I'm not comprehending what I'm hearing."

Oh, yes, I know! I know that! Thank God somebody told you! I thought.

Before UMAP, communication with Ted was quite difficult. I'd say something to Ted like, "You know you have a doctor's appointment tomorrow, right?"

And he'd say, "What are you saying? You're not making any sense."

"I am making sense."

"No, you're not. First you said something different."

"I'm reminding you that you have a doctor's appointment tomorrow," I'd say.

"You never told me that."

"Yes, I did."

I knew he wasn't fully comprehending what I was trying to tell him, but he thought he was, because in his mind, he heard the words and knew what he wanted to say. He had disconnects between his ears and his brain, and between his brain and his mouth.

Thankfully, part of Joy's job in helping him improve was to be honest. She told him, "You know Ted, you're not always comprehending things. You're not always understanding what people are saying to you."

That night at dinner was one of the few times I ever saw him cry about what had happened to him because of the stroke.

He tried to tell me that he had communicated effectively and clearly to Joy about his day with the therapists. That is what I presumed from his speech. But I knew (and Joy knew) his ability to communicate and his comprehension were broken.

Even though that was scary, it was a pivotal moment for him. He had severe expressive aphasia, so he knew he had difficulty with speech. Now, he realized that hearing and comprehending were also hard.

On My Own

On day two at UMAP, I told Kelly I'd see her around, and she went home to Chicago with our pug. I'd been walking Sullivan mornings and evenings since we bought him. With both of them gone, I knew my life was going to get even worse. I would be alone in Ann Arbor.

I'd have to meet new friends. I'd have to take a bus to the facility from the hotel. I'd have to figure out how to get dinner every night.

Those simple things weren't simple for me. I was on my own for the first time since my stroke. I didn't want to eat in the hotel every night, but I couldn't go to the grocery store for food that I would have to prepare, because I didn't have any kitchen appliances—or even a kitchenette. So, I just sat there in my room contemplating and feeling sad. It was a far cry from what I used to do. I remembered when I worked and had to talk to so many people during the day to build relationships and do my job successfully.

The second or third time I went to Joy's office, she pulled out a *Wall Street Journal*. She said, "What is the interest rate today? What is it doing?"

I said, "Up."

She said, "Okay, explain that to me. Use one or two verbs." She knew that I used to work in the finance industry, so she knew I read *The Wall Street Journal* before the stroke.

"What stock exchanges am I talking about? Dow Jones or NAS-DAQ?" she asked.

I had to relearn those words. I had to really study every day.

I had to meet with Joy for fifteen to thirty minutes every morning at UMAP, and she'd ask me these kinds of questions every day. She knew this was the best way to get to me. Getting me to use those financial terms helped me improve sentences and regain words.

The UMAP program was great—and intensive. It ran from nine in the morning to four in the afternoon. It was a grind, but I knew I needed it.

I had speech therapy twice every morning and once every afternoon. One session was private, and the other two were small group therapy sessions with three or four people. I was with the same group of people in these sessions for the six weeks that I was there.

Two or three days every week, UMAP also ran a music program and slotted me to attend. We sang "Happy Birthday" almost every time I was in music therapy. If it wasn't someone's birthday in the program, then we would sing "Happy Birthday" to a famous person whose birthday it happened to be that day.

I was supposed to get up there and try to sing. But I didn't. I couldn't sing. That was one thing I simply could not do. Even to this day, I can't sing, but I can hum. I decided there were only twenty-four hours in every day, and my time would be better spent elsewhere. If I wasn't trying to sing, I could be doing other things. I went back to Joy.

"I have to change sessions," I attempted to tell her. "Let me go back to learning pictures and looking at verbs and nouns," I pleaded as best I could. She did understand, but she didn't agree. So, I continued to try to sing "Happy Birthday."

They also put me in a daily art program. I walked into the room with some hesitancy. It was a fairly large room with several tables. On one of the tables was a pile of magazines. I was immediately intimidated seeing so much written information. It overwhelmed me.

"Look through the magazines and pick one of the dream cars you could see yourself owning," the therapist instructed.

I picked something like a Maserati or a Lamborghini.

The therapist said, "All right. Do you remember this? Do you know what this is called?"

I tried, but I couldn't answer. I couldn't even remember what a Chevy was. Finally, I said, "It's not a Ford." At least I gave an answer . . . but something else also happened. At that moment, and I didn't realize this at the time, I subconsciously started a different way of communicating. I looked for new words, rather than leaning on words that I should have known. About half of the time most people would understand what I was trying to say, and therapists would usually get it perfectly.

Unlike the therapy I had at RIC in the hospital and in Northbrook, where the therapists moved from group to group every day and sometimes client to another client, I saw the same therapists every day at UMAP, which was fantastic. They got to know each patient's progress, and they would report back to Joy every day. My therapist knew what I was struggling with in particular and could pick up where she left off the day before, as opposed to coming in cold every single day and having no idea where I was in my recovery. We were also able to review the words or the articles of speech that we had discussed the time before.

It's not that the therapy one institution provided was better than another. They were all working toward achieving one goal—helping me get better. It was up to me to pick which type of therapy I liked. For me, it was best to take notes, study, review, and repeat information over and over with the same teacher. Due to my prognosis at that point, I needed this type of therapy. Someone else in my situation may need something different.

My therapists weren't too hard on me and didn't force me to do anything I was having trouble with, but anything I had a problem with was noted so it could be addressed later.

"Car, tire, road," she said after that. "Try to remember these words—car, tire, road." Then, as if she hadn't mentioned them, she moved on to the day's assignment. When the day's lesson was finished, though, she came back to these words.

"Okay, now we're going to move back. You know those three nouns I told you to remember at the start of our session? What were they?"

I didn't know. It was so frustrating. Having gone through this program, I learned from Dr. Taber, my neurologist, that my brain had not yet reorganized itself. The nouns and verbs would come into my brain but leave just as quickly. In order to retain them, I had to practice and stay focused.

Getting with the Program

I got into a routine at UMAP, and I liked my therapy sessions very much. I had breakfast with my group, and then we had therapy together. After therapy, we would break for lunch. Afternoons involved more therapy, a break, the last of the day's activities, and then a return to our hotels.

I had lunch every day with nine other stroke survivors, and we all had different problems associated with aphasia. My speech was focused on nouns and trying to memorize them. Sometimes, I spoke broken phrases with few (if any) verbs. I would try to have conversations with them, to explain what happened to me—the stroke, RIC, the surgeries, and so on. The youngest two of the group had caregivers, who were probably their mothers, with them.

It was a tough time for me. I had trouble adjusting to the UMAP program, especially because my stroke was so recent.

In one of our therapy sessions, I played computer games to see if I could identify synonyms. In another, we read and discussed simple books, like *Curious George*. The therapists were young and fun, and they had a lot of patience. But still, I got frustrated during the sessions. They'd say, "Take it easy. Take your time." They would set me up with a joke, and even if I couldn't answer with the punch line, at least I was getting it—I could comprehend the joke and laugh about it.

There was a lot of repetition within the therapy programs at UMAP, but in a good way. I would learn, review, and repeat many of the exercises over and over again. To a person who hasn't had a stroke, the exercises would seem straightforward and simple.

For instance, I had to learn, review, and repeat the following chart every other day to help me learn verb tenses:

SUBJECT (WHO?)	VERB (WHAT?)	LOCATION (WHERE?)	TIME (WHEN?)
I	eat ate will eat	at home	Monday
My family	watch TV watched TV will watch TV	in New York	this evening
My friend	is going went will go	at the store	Saturday
The man	works out worked out will work out	at the gym	at night

"Where did you guys go for dinner last night?" the therapist would ask. We all had to find the words that connected with the questions they asked.

And someone in the program would raise their hand and then respond, "Yeah, okay, where we went last night was the restaurant by the hotel."

That wasn't me. I wasn't the guy who raised his hand during these discussions, where there were a lot of people around the table. I was still learning, recovering my speech. I liked UMAP's aphasia group participation, but I could neither keep up nor participate in these general discussions.

"Ted, tell me where you went last night," said one of the therapists, but I couldn't use the right words, and I couldn't formulate sentences. And, they couldn't stop the flow to let me find the words, because one hour would turn into three. So, they would say, "That's okay. We'll come back to that question." And thanks to the excellent therapists, conversation kept flowing.

We had many book discussions and also discussions about the program in general. We sat around a big table with the therapists and their bosses—the people who taught the therapists—on one side and about five of us stroke survivors on the other side. We discussed what we thought about the books we were reading. We also shared our views of the UMAP programs—what we liked and what we didn't like.

One of the most useful parts of UMAP, I found, was that I had a chance to build a rapport with the therapists there. They got to know me; they spent time with me. At the hospital in Chicago and other programs, the speech therapists rotated so often that it was hard to truly see my improvement.

At UMAP, they were knowledgeable, and they cared. It made a big difference in my recovery.

Finding a Friend

There was one guy in the program with aphasia who I got along with really well. His name was Tom Hilgendorf, and he was from Texas.

The first time I met Tom, he asked me about what happened with my stroke and where I lived. I responded as clearly as I could, and he was able to understand part of it. Then I asked him, in broken English, "How many times have you been in this program?"

Tom understood what I was asking him and said, "I think twice before."

It was something I started doing at every therapy program; I'd find someone to interact with every day and see how well they understood me. It was a way to measure my progress, and I'd do it with different people throughout the day. At first, I targeted only others with aphasia, but soon, I began approaching people without.

The first time I met Tom, he invited me to dinner.

There will be more conversation. I am already tired. I have to look at the homework before bed, I thought.

The truth was that I wasn't ready for a full dinner conversation yet.

"Can't," I said, and I went back to my room, got my book and pictures, and practiced my homework. I guess it was my desire to get through this program and regain the words, the articles of speech, the colloquial sayings—all the language I had lost. I didn't know if this program could fix my speech entirely, though that is what I had hoped. But I crashed when faced with certain hurdles, like the prospect of having to carry on a conversation through dinner. It hadn't occurred to me how difficult it would be to relearn English, or how slow that process would be.

When I got back to my hotel room each night, I would pace. I walked across the hotel room, to the window, then to the table, and then back again. Sometimes, the room would close in on me. I didn't particularly like sitting alone in my room at the hotel every evening or eating in the hotel every night, but what else was I supposed to do?

Tom asked me to dinner two or three more times, and by the end of my second week at UMAP, I took him up on the offer. We went to Applebee's. For him, to explain our situation to the waitress was unbelievably tough. He was way better at it than I was, though. I had to point at the menu. The waiters were patient, which was good for us.

I didn't want to eat alone every night, but I also didn't want to go out with somebody every night. When I ate alone, I had time to get back to my homework. But I realized after about a month in this program that in order to get better at speaking, I'd have to socialize. It didn't really matter who I talked to. I just had to put my toe in the water. Those days were difficult for me . . . ordering a cup of coffee at Starbucks, asking a stranger for directions, or interacting with the cashier at the grocery store. And I didn't take for granted, for example, that I could go to Starbucks and order a latte without practicing beforehand. I guess it was the situation I was in—aphasia, UMAP, trying to regain my speech. Interacting with strangers was great practice for me. I developed unscripted exercises and used them frequently. And eventually, they worked!

CHAPTER 13

Setback . . . a Seizure?

About three weeks into my six-week stay at UMAP, I decided to rent a car. Now technically, I was not allowed to rent, or even drive, a car, but I obviously wasn't going to let that stop me.

Unfortunately, this is when a lot of things went wrong.

I had been taking the UMAP bus that was designated for people with aphasia to and from UMAP every day. When I got back to the hotel, I'd drive to the YMCA to work out for an hour and a half. The people at UMAP knew I was going to the YMCA. The people at the YMCA got to know me.

My wife didn't know about the car or the YMCA.

Kelly

I remember calling him and saying, "How was your day?"

And he said, "Oh, good."

"What'd you do?"

"Surprise."

"A surprise? For me?" I asked.

"No."

"You got a surprise for you?"

"Uh-huh."

"What is it?"

"Green."

"Green? Did you buy a backpack to carry your cards and papers to UMAP?"

He started laughing. Then he said, "Hertz."

And I said, "What? Did you rent a car?"

"Yeah."

"Somebody let you rent a car?" I thought, *Oh my gosh, a green car. I'm thinking of something like a backpack, a bag, and instead he's gone and rented a car!*

I couldn't stop him from doing things like that, and I honestly didn't want to, because that's Ted, and he had already come so far in his recovery doing things his own way. I wasn't going to micromanage him and tell him he couldn't. He needed to do that; he needed that independence. How do you go from being an executive to being told, by your wife, that you can't drive a car?

Sometimes, I did say things like, "Ted, you shouldn't be doing that." But I couldn't stop him. In fact, he thought it was hilarious. I could hear the gears turning in his head: *As soon as she leaves and drives back to Chicago, I'm going to Hertz!*

That's so Ted.

--- --- ---

The rental associate from Hertz took my lack of speech to mean I was a foreigner, and I didn't bother attempting a different explanation. I gave him my identification to review and signed many insurance papers. Then, I took the car and ran!

Actually, I was quite careful with the rented car. I drove it slowly to the YMCA gym. It took about ten or fifteen minutes to get there.

I was careful with my workout at the gym, too. I did a little exercise regimen that included stretching and using the StairMaster.

What messed me up, though, was that I did my regimen without any food or water in my system on that particular day.

It was a Saturday, but I had returned to my old ways, in a sense. That meant that I went to the gym every day, even on the weekends, and coming in early on a Saturday morning meant that the gym was nearly absent of people, so I had my choice of machines. I headed for the StairMaster, and warmed up for a couple of minutes before increasing my pace to my typical workout speed.

Suddenly, the music playing in the background grew fuzzy.

Ow! My scream echoed through my head as a painful sensation like a jolt of electricity shot through it.

I grabbed for the handle of the StairMaster, but my hand kept slipping. Suddenly, I was spinning, or at least my head was.

I'm going to pass out. Just grab the handle. Grab the handle, I thought. But I couldn't, I blacked out, and my head slammed to the floor.

When the paramedics arrived, my thoughts were clear, or that's what I thought. Later, I found out that I had not been thinking clearly at all, and my answers and comments to the paramedics and doctors were a little off.

I hadn't eaten breakfast that morning. I had only had a cup of coffee and a little water. I thought that maybe this is what caused me to black out and fall. I wondered if dehydration was to blame. I complained of a small headache near my left forehead.

I told the paramedics that I had baseline speech expressive aphasia. And at the time, my speech seemed normal—normal in the sense that it was as it had been the past few weeks and no worse.

I was taken to the University of Michigan Medical Center emergency room and kept in the hospital for a day, and I was allowed to go home that night. I didn't think the incident was a big deal at all.

As it turned out, I'd had a seizure. I was out for fifteen minutes rather than four or five minutes, as I had initially thought. My thinking it wasn't a big deal meant that I didn't realize what had happened. I wasn't comprehending.

I called Kelly that night when I got home and explained to her what had happened in the gym, as best as I could.

"Oh my God, did you have another stroke?" she asked.

"No. No stroke. Seizure," I tried to respond. "It didn't feel like anything. I just blacked out."

"But was it a stroke, Ted? Did it do more damage?" Clearly, she was understanding little of what I was saying, even though it sounded normal to me. So, it was a guessing game, which was frustrating for both of us. We both knew we had come further than this in our ability to communicate, and now it felt like we were back at square one. How had this happened?

When I got back to the program on Monday, my therapists knew about the seizure and asked me what had happened. They were compassionate and kept asking me if I was all right.

After the seizure, I lost some of the words and phrases I had regained. It took a lot of energy to focus on saying words and forming phrases again.

Dr. Taber had warned me months ago that I was going to have seizures, but I hadn't understood what that meant at the time. He said seizures were common after a brain injury.

When we spoke again, after my seizure, he said, "Your brain is like Jell-O right now, Ted. It's healing, but it hasn't stabilized itself yet. Now that you have had one seizure, it is even more likely that you'll have another."

This guy had the ability to predict things like this. He was an oracle, and I was thankful to have him as my neurologist.

After the seizure at UMAP, I thought, *Okay, now I know what's going to happen, so I'll be very careful if the sensation I felt happens again. I can help the recovery of my brain, like having more water, especially in the morning. But if I can't stop the seizure from happening, then I'm just going to accept it and keep pushing on through.* So that's what I did.

CHAPTER 14

I Decided to Win

After I finished my six-week stint in UMAP in February of 2006, I returned to Chicago and resumed my therapy sessions with Melissa at RIC. I also reached out to the speech clinic of Northwestern University and contacted Doreen Kelly Izaguirre, the speech therapist Melissa recommended before I went to UMAP. Kelly had decided to go to school to get a bachelor's degree and was busy with classes during the day. We lived so close to RIC in the city that I could walk there twice per week for physical therapy and to speech therapy at RIC with Melissa.

I returned to Chicago with a new attitude. The twenty-four-month mark since my stroke was approaching all too quickly. Twenty-four months was when the doctors told me that learning and regaining my abilities would plateau, but I only saw this idea that I would plateau as a challenge. And, after a long, hard rehab, reflecting and contemplating, I seized it! This would only be the beginning of my recovery. I knew I would continue to grow.

Nevertheless, time was on my mind, so I stopped going to physical therapy at RIC in the city. I joined a gym, got a trainer, and worked out every day at six thirty a.m., pushing myself for up to an hour and a half. On the days I went to Northwestern, I'd be done with speech therapy around two in the afternoon, so I'd spend some more time in the gym, and then I'd get acupuncture.

Funny enough, the acupuncturist I saw wasn't sure he could help me at first. He was from China, and his English was not so good. Understanding each other was a challenge, but if we could find a place in the middle, we could sometimes have a good conversation. That was yet another outlet for me to get better at speaking. He said he'd try to help, but he wasn't sure how much it would improve my speech. But when I told him about my seizures, he lit up. "I can definitely help you with that," he said. "Now I know where we're going to go. If I can work on the flow in your brain, it will help your speech get better and help to prevent further seizures."

Soon, my speech was progressively getting better, though I couldn't say what was helping most. Acupuncture? Running the treadmill at the gym? More therapy?

"Ted?" Kelly said with surprise one evening as we sat talking.

"What?" I answered.

"Your speech . . ."

"What?" I asked again, confused by what she was trying to say, a little nervous.

"It seems . . . it's so much better. I just realized that it's always better on the days that you go to the gym, when you run on the treadmill."

My nervousness dissipated and was replaced with happiness. It made me feel good to hear her say that.

About the time I started seeing the acupuncturist, I also started using Earobics, which was software for language learning. It had lots of games with names like Memory Matrix, Rhyme Time, and Sound Check. One of the most useful games was one where I had to listen for subtle differences in similar words—for instance, clean and clan or fan and phone. Another program called Parrot worked on building strategies for getting the correct word out. Often with aphasia, you know what you want to say, but you can't say it or you say it incorrectly. Parrot helped me think of the first letter, describe the item or action, and associate the word with other words to help recover that language skill and say the correct word. I learned that if I couldn't remember the correct word, I could describe it in other ways to get my point across. These games were extremely helpful.

Kelly

Ted's favorite therapist from UMAP, Joy, had sent Ted home with a four-inch binder full of exercises, and of course, Ted did them. He went through each page of that binder and did the exercises over and over again. She gave him other things to do to enhance his communication skills, too.

Ted really likes working with smart, competent people, and he will find them. He loved Joy. He respected her, and she really helped him, even after he came back from UMAP. In fact, he went up to Michigan when she opened her private practice there and worked with her for a week.

– – –

I finally joined the Aphasia Club at RIC in the city, which met twice a week, on Tuesdays and Thursdays. As I listened to others tell their stories there, I heard the same struggles in them that I had been contending with. *If I get better, so much better that nobody knows that I have aphasia, I can help people like this*, I thought.

That was my intermediate goal. It wasn't like I wanted to be a public speaker. I was aiming for small goals that turned into medium goals, before I got to the big goals. I also participated in research experiments set up by the aphasia director at RIC. I sat in front of a computer, listened to someone talk, and then repeated the sentences I heard. Every time I went through one of those six-week experiments, my speech got a little better. With each experiment, I focused on different details that I needed to work on. First, I worked on nouns and second, verbs. Then, I tried to memorize and say an entire fragment and then a sentence. And then, I tried to improve the intonation of my speech and so on and so on.

We'd also practice simple scripts written by the therapists and based generally on our own life experiences. We would try to memorize them, placing a lot of focus on the key points of the short conversations. For instance, the script might go something like this:

You: Nice to meet you. Are you from New York originally?
Mary: Oh no. I moved here from Boston. I transferred jobs.

In this example, I would try to focus on the "from New York originally." In doing these exercises, we learned to converse more freely and to work on the tone and content of our questions. And, by emphasizing certain words and phrases, we could get the point across, even if the other words failed us. So, for example:

You: Well, it was nice to talk to you.
Mary: Okay. Bye.

If I couldn't remember the full two sentences, then I focused on the key points. I could, at the very least, say, "Nice talking," which would get my meaning across.

Maximizing My Rehab

Sometime during 2007, the neurologists and stroke doctors I talked to at RIC told me it was time to think about my left vs. the right side of my brain. There was a portion in the left hemisphere that I didn't have anymore. At least, that was their hypothesis. And for me, I would try anything to get my speech better.

"You'll build neurons that will go around the dead cells, but that will take some time," I was told. "You'll learn that your right brain will begin to compensate. You'll find new ways to do things, and you'll do them with the right hemisphere of your brain."

When I went to UMAP, I couldn't do math and I had trouble figuring out simple things—getting from point A to point B. Those are usually left-brained tasks. I had to figure out how to work those kinds of things out using the right hemisphere of my brain and maybe by using some connections that I had on the right side of my brain in a different way. It was a little slower, but it would work.

I rented a car on Mondays and Wednesdays (which nobody knew about, including my wife) to get to Northwestern University Speech Clinic in Evanston, where I had two types of therapy. The first was one-on-one, but they approached therapy differently. They introduced new techniques during these sessions.

One day, the therapist greeted me and then said, "Okay, I'm going to put on CNN on my laptop. Listen to what the newscaster says in this clip, and then summarize it for me." It sounds simple, but it was tough for me. "Can you tell me in one or two sentences about what you just learned?" the therapist would ask. They would want me to summarize the clip with words like, "This is a clip about—" This is easy for me now, but at the time, it was frustrating and difficult.

I simply looked at her for a moment and realized that I couldn't. "No. Do it again," I responded, and we watched it all over again.

I was still relearning how to put nouns and verbs together and how to access the parts of my memory I'd lost. Pronouns, adverbs, and prepositions were still out of my reach, but my comprehension of the overall gist of the clip seemed to get better. Having to regain the ability to memorize the minute details of English, on top of learning nouns, verbs, and so on, was a tall order. But I knew I could conquer this. Eventually, I began to build new pathways in my brain. I had to practice, practice, practice!

The other type of therapy was in a group setting that focused on synonyms and definitions. Instead of asking us to name an object or picture—which none of us could remember—the therapist would say, "What are the characteristics of this word? Is it big or small? What shape is it? Or just describe what you think this is."

It was a way of getting to the actual definition of words, such as *eyeglasses* or *toaster*. We couldn't remember the name of the object, but we could figure out what it did, how it worked, and what it was used for. In one exercise, I listened to a therapist who was talking to another patient. The therapist had a coffee cup in his hand, and he said, "I want you to describe this. What do you think it is? Is it a circle? Is it tall or small?"

The patient said, "That's a drinking container." He definitely got it, but as a person who has aphasia he could find a better noun in this exercise, like *coffee cup*.

This may seem like a small, small task, but for people who have this type of aphasia, this is a great achievement. And for me, it challenged me to explain things as succinctly as I could. That meant, eventually, that I would practice multiple definitions for the same word or item so I could describe it more fluently.

There were many benefits of doing this exercise. My brain is always on and thinking of different ways to say the same thing, because you don't know when you will forget a word. And I picked up a few tips, such as how to keep a conversation moving by using different words when I forgot the actual word I wanted to use. Everybody does this, but since I have aphasia, I had to work double time to come up with alternative words.

Another technique we used at Northwestern was the book club. One of my favorite books was *Water for Elephants*, a historical novel by Sara Gruen. We had to read a specified number of pages each week and then review them as a group. The therapists would ask us to read a paragraph out loud. I was one of five stroke survivors sitting on one side of a table. Three clinicians from the Northwestern speech program sat on the other side of the table with a list of questions they wanted to ask us. Eventually, I was able to ask them at least two questions every week. That was a switch for the clinicians!

On Tuesdays and Thursdays, I went to the RIC Aphasia Book Club, where I was reading another book, *A Reporter's Life* by Walter Cronkite. The book clubs at Northwestern and RIC kept me busy. This process of reading and understanding a book, trying to summarize the chapters, and saying it aloud was extremely crucial for me. It was an effective therapy technique, and I was glad I had finally joined in. I joined at the right time for me. Putting all the things I had learned so far in cohesive, succinct sentences, without errors, was the goal.

So, I set up my schedule every week to participate in these groups, which were both quite difficult. I was reading four chapters, in total, per week—two from *Water for Elephants* and two from *A Reporter's Life*. I got through them, but I didn't necessarily comprehend what I was reading. I wasn't sure, for example, what Walter Cronkite did on a particular day. I had to reread portions of the book three times to finally get it. But I did the work and stayed current with the group. As time went by, I could see myself making progress.

For a while, I participated in various book clubs—both leading a book group and participating in various others—and I found there are many benefits to accrue (reading, comprehending, summarizing). Over the next year, while a member of these various book clubs, I read *90 Minutes in Heaven, The Alchemist, In Cold Blood, The Memory Keeper's Daughter, Left Neglected, The Harbinger, The Monk Who Sold His Ferrari, The Boy in the Suitcase, Kill Me If You Can, Taken, The Uninvited Guest*, and my favorite so far, *Gang Leader for a Day*.

In addition to joining these book clubs, I decided to start private therapy sessions with Doreen Kelly Izaguirre, which were totally different from the others. I had left her a voice message in October 2005, before Kelly and I went up to visit UMAP. When I came back to Chicago and started working with Doreen, she said she could tell that my speech had gotten much better—significantly better—since leaving her that voice message. It was such a slow progression that I hadn't been aware of the difference.

With Doreen, I did unstructured supported conversation, the most common form of speech therapy.

Doreen

As a speech pathologist, I take patients at any stage of the game, no matter what level they are working on. It was Ted's choice to go to UMAP first. He wanted to take advantage of their intensive program.

I could see Ted's progression immediately when he reached out again after he got back. He left a voice mail for me before he left for UMAP. Being a therapist, I knew what he was asking in the voice mail, even though his sentences and phrases were broken. Then, when I heard from him again after he came back from UMAP, the change was unbelievable. It was mind-boggling! I wish I had saved the initial voice mail to show his level of progression and as evidence of how determined he was.

The thing that impressed me most about Ted was that he came into every therapy session with an agenda. He'd say, "Here's what I want to be able to do. Here's what's hard for me. Here's an example of what I tried to do and couldn't."

We worked on all aspects of language, whether it was word finding or sentence structure. There were many times when we were literally mapping out sentence structure because that was the part of Ted's language that was impaired. We even did some scripting therapy. He would say—and again, he was saying this through more of an aphasic-style language—"When I'm out socially, I just want to make small talk." He wanted some prepared things to say about sports, movies, or the weather and then, eventually, current events, which meant he was challenging himself with adding more complex ideas to build richer sentences.

It's hard to describe our therapeutic sessions. He would say something, I would write down what he said, we would restructure the sentence and either focus on nouns or focus on verbs, and then we would put those words in sentences.

He took such ownership of his program. He was always working on speaking better. Before his stroke, he was such a successful, brilliant man, and then to have this happen . . .

Most people, when learning about aphasia, don't understand it; they don't always understand that for patients with aphasia, it's more of a communication issue. It's hard to understand that they have their intellectual faculties and know what they want to say, but they don't have the ability to communicate it.

But then when there's that struggle to get out something so simple to someone who doesn't understand it, they think, *Oh, he might be confused. Let me do it for him; let me say it for him.* This was so frustrating for Ted, who couldn't communicate the way he used to.

He's a very take-charge guy. He takes on the attitude of *I will make this work, and this is how.*

That was another thing that impressed me about Ted from day one—he explored so many different options for therapy early on. He pursued all of these on his own, and many of them he would pay for privately. I think he probably looked at that the way he would invest in any business. His attitude was that he was making an investment, and he was going to direct it, control it, and get the most out of it. And it was fantastic because he brought real-world issues into his therapy sessions, which was great.

When we talk about aphasia in a patient's early days after the diagnosis, it's huge. Everything about your life is the aphasia. The goal is to slowly shrink it, so that life is bigger than the aphasia. The aphasia is a component, sure, but it's getting to be smaller and smaller. Ted worked so hard at that. He's still working at it and doing fantastic.

- - -

"What're you doing?" Kelly asked one evening as I sat at the table with a stack of index cards. "Where'd you get those?"

"Store," I answered and went back to the task at hand. My handwriting was rough. I wrote simple conversational sentences, one sentence for each index card, and I didn't know what would happen, but I wanted to take more control over my speech. I was beginning to formulate a project plan for my recovery, though I didn't even realize it at the time.

The first month after I started writing on the index cards, which then became writing on the computer, my writing got better than my speech did. Then the next month, it switched, and my speech grew by a larger margin. The following month, my handwriting leapfrogged my speech again.

"It makes sense, Ted. They are interrelated—one affects the other," Doreen told me in one of our sessions.

That hadn't occurred to me. Suddenly, I knew I had to strategize to get the most growth in both areas.

At the next session, she opened the door to welcome me into her office and noted the book in my hand. "What is that, Ted? A dictionary?"

"Yes," I replied.

I started toting the dictionary around with me wherever I went. When I had a few free moments, like when I was waiting for a therapist, I would take it out and choose five new words to remember. Then I would work on them, over and over again, in my head. Five words every day. As I write this book, I'm still adding two or three words to my vocabulary daily. That's how I continue to get my speech back.

All of Column A, All of Column B

I am restless by nature, so I developed my own rehab program, adding anything I thought would help. There was always a purpose for doing a specific exercise; I needed to know why and how an exercise would benefit me before I did it. I had been worried, after my stroke, that I had lost my gift, but I realized that this *was* my gift—not accounting or finance but determination and motivation. Working to reach a goal and beating the odds were my gifts, and they worked for me during my recovery as they had in my career.

In October of 2008, I took an English class that met for three hours twice a week, for eight weeks. I was one of twenty people in the class, and I decided that I would not tell the teacher I had aphasia. He went through the parts of speech: One session was nouns and verbs, another was pronouns, and so on. It was like an English as a second language (ESL) class, only some of the people were just there to study the language. For me, it was a separate, nontherapeutic way to interact with other people while we all learned the same things. I could practice my language, but I could also work on my social skills.

I liked the challenge of the ESL approach, so I talked to Sherrie Malleis, who ran the Loyola University ESL department in Chicago, and added her as a "therapist" too. She was patient, she listened to what I was trying to convey, and she was excellent at teaching language. She gave me a lot of strategies and tactics to get my thoughts, or a description of a story, "across the table" in conversation.

When I was in high school, my dad taught me about the importance of getting a job and how much is required of you to attain a great job and the best quality of life. That translates in my hard work in rehab and now in recovery. Changing the metrics a bit. Eventually, I realized the hard work I put in toward being able to speak and write again, socializing, and coming back to the community is paying off. As long as I refine and continue my progress, it becomes second nature. Enjoyment!

CHAPTER 15

No More Limits

I n the fall of 2007, Kelly and I found out about an experimental aphasia program at the Veterans Administration (VA) in Orlando, near the University of Central Florida. They offered a four-week program with individual and specialized aphasia therapy. I figured it would be good for me, so I gave it a try. I stayed at the Embassy Suites and walked to the gym at the University of Central Florida every day to get some exercise.

While I was at the gym each day, I worked with a therapist from the VA for three or four hours. It wasn't an official part of the aphasia program at UCF, but the therapist worked with me and another guy who had a speech impediment. Every morning, the staff would greet us as we came in.

"How are you doing?" they would say and wait for us to respond. Then they'd note our responses and compare them to our previous responses to track our progress.

With one therapist, we played hands-on games, like word searches and go fish, which let the therapist evaluate us as we went through the processes. She then gave us a report on how we did at the end of each session.

I had never played games before as part of therapy. These sessions consisted of one clinician to two patients, rather than the more common one-on-one or group dynamics, and a different kind of therapeutic approach. The thing was, I couldn't devote myself to this therapeutic approach. Unlike the other programs I'd been in, I was alone, despite being paired with another patient, because I was the only one in this setting with aphasia. I thought I would get used to it and develop my social and listening skills while building a comradeship with the other patient, but I never did.

"How was it?" Kelly wanted to know when I got back.

"No good," I answered, though that wasn't entirely true. Every therapy I've tried has had some value. They all challenged me in various ways. But I was lonely in Florida. And I did not like that.

After returning from the program at UCF, I immediately got back into my routine in Chicago: the Aphasia Club, the Book Club, and going to Northwestern University twice a week for therapy. Part of what I did at Northwestern was to participate in experiments that were created by students who were going to the school in Northwestern's doctorate program. They had to do a certain number of experiments with stroke survivors.

In one of these experiments, they would show me pictures of people doing an activity and then say the verb tense of whatever it was the people were doing—swim, running, walk, drove, eat, been sleeping. Then, I'd have to repeat the verb, tell what tense it was, and use that verb in a complete sentence. It was hard and frustrating, but it was a great exercise for me at that point in my recovery.

And that was only one experiment; there were many others. When they discovered that one of these techniques had positive results in stroke survivors with aphasia, they would share it with other aphasia centers who belonged to an aphasia network, such as RIC and San Diego State University.

Throwing My Own Switch

Many PhDs that I met during my recovery said that if your stroke affected your right side of your body, as mine did, you should do everything on the left, but that never made any sense to me. I wanted to regain full use and strength of my right side, and I couldn't do that by always using my left.

I read *The Wall Street Journal* every morning. It's a tough newspaper, and I still didn't get everything immediately, but I read through it. When I walked to RIC in the city, I would make sure I held my newspaper on my right side. I also started wearing my watch on my right wrist and shaved with my right hand. Eventually, I took it even further.

One night early in my recovery (about one month after I was released from inpatient RIC), I came home to a wonderful smell in the kitchen, lamb chops. Kelly knew that it was one of my favorite meals, and she was quite happy to see my smile. I sat down, mouth watering at the familiar food, and picked up my fork with my left hand. Then suddenly, my smile faded. My right arm wouldn't cooperate. I couldn't pick up my knife with my right hand to enjoy the meal. I couldn't even feed myself my favorite food.

I was stubborn and didn't want to ruin the special meal, so I switched hands, attempting to cut the lamb chops with my left hand. Much like the child who tries to write with the nondominant hand, my efforts were sloppy and awkward. The full weight of the realization that I was handicapped came crashing down on me, and tears blurred my vision. When at last I was able to wipe them away enough to look up, I saw Kelly wiping her own eyes.

"I'm so sorry, Ted. This was supposed to be special. I didn't know . . . ," she said, but I cut her off with a wave of my hand. I wiped harder at my eyes.

"It'll get better. It will, Ted. It will get better," she reassured me. I knew she was right, but it wasn't going to get better on its own. I had to take charge. And that's exactly what I did.

One day not too long after the lamb chop incident, I took a small rope and said to Kelly, "Tie this."

"What are you doing?" she asked as she tied my left hand behind my back.

"Today, I'll eat dinner with my right hand, and after that, I'll use that side of my body until I am ready to go to bed. I'm trying to get better."

Once I felt like I was improving, I'd switch to the left side. I began alternating between my left and right side each day. It gave me a different way of firing the neurons in my brain by switching from the right brain to the left brain and back again. I was building new synaptic pathways to replace the ones I'd lost. I talked to some of the PhDs at Northwestern about it, and they said they had never thought about it like that; no one had ever done anything like that before. But I did it for the entire first year of my recovery, and my right side improved. Now, nobody can tell which side of my body was impacted by the stroke.

It's all about motivation, mind, and determination. I figured if I really wanted to do something, it was up to me to do it. There was no prescription or set therapy, no panacea that would fix the issues I wanted fixed. All anyone would tell me was, "Wait until later," or "Oh, you can't do that," or "You're disabled, so deal with it." I'm glad I didn't listen to them, and I hope that people who think they can't make these kinds of changes are reading this. There is hope, and there are ways to change!

But no one knew what was going on in my head, and the doctors didn't know what I could and couldn't take on. They only knew what they were trained to say.

That's why I did it. It was my body and my life, and I wanted to be in control. The word *no* has never been a part of my equation.

Kelly

I don't think I've ever met anyone who is as focused and determined as Ted is. I tell people, "You don't understand—this guy doesn't procrastinate. He's very strategic. He's great with time management. He's clever. He's extremely results oriented."

People will say, "Yeah, I think I know somebody like that."

And I think, *No, not like Ted.* He got frustrated during his recovery, but he never got angry. He wasn't a quitter. *He will find a way to recover.*

"Do you ever wonder why this happened to you?" I'd asked him.

"I can't think about that; I've just got to move forward," he would answer.

Every night at dinner, we would talk about the stroke—not necessarily the events of the stroke, but the rehab. The speech therapy, the physical therapy, what happened with it. That was the focal point of our conversations.

"I'm sad, aren't you?" I would ask him.

He would say—not as fluidly as I'm putting it now, but he'd make me understand—"I can't be sad. I can't let myself get to that point. It can't get me anywhere."

I guess that was his way of coping so he could keep moving forward. In a way, he was sad and somewhat depressed, but overall, many people who have brain injuries, like a stroke or a traumatic brain injury, have depression issues. He didn't. He had down days where he was a little blue, but that's normal; we all have those. But he did not go through any major depression like a lot of stroke survivors do.

Remarkable? Yeah. Ted's personality never changed, thank God. He's just as driven as he always was.

No Fun in Arizona

"Let's try to use our timeshare at the resort in Scottsdale or we're going to lose it," Kelly said to me one morning. "It'd be fun to get away."

"Okay," I replied.

"Okay? You're okay with me scheduling it?"

"Yes," I said.

"All right," she said with a smile. "I'll call today."

We took an early flight. I was extremely tired, and it's a long stretch from the airport terminal to the gate.

"Do you want me to get someone to help us? Maybe one of those carts?" Kelly asked.

I said no quite emphatically. I wanted to walk through the airport. I always walked. I had a disabled placard for my car in Chicago, but I never used it. Still, by the time we got to the gate, I was exhausted.

"Are you okay?" Kelly asked me.

"Yes," I answered her. She would ask several more times before we touched down in Scottsdale.

"Are you sure that you're okay?"

"Yes."

"But, you're limping, Ted," Kelly answered the final time as we made our way out of the airport.

The next morning at the hotel, the kind surrounded by golf courses, I woke up bright and early, but Kelly wanted to sleep in.

"Go to sleep, Ted. Get some rest," she muttered and then rolled over.

"Can't sleep. Need coffee," I said and then started for the lobby. It was about seven a.m. when I left our room, which was like a casita.

Walking down the path, on my way to the front desk, I spotted a gym in our hotel. No one was in there that early, so I decided to exercise for forty-five minutes. I didn't have a water bottle, but they had a fountain with little cups, so I was able to have a little water. Then, I continued my walk.

I found the front desk and asked, "Coffee?"

"No. I'm sorry," the receptionist answered. "There's a coffee maker in your room though, sir." She gave me an apologetic smile, and I walked away.

There was a spread of breakfast foods being set out for a conference. I saw a banana and took it as I walked by. I was sorry to see they were still grinding the coffee, so I opened the door to take the path back around the outdoor pool and toward my room.

That's when my body froze. My face locked; I couldn't move my jaw. I fell down on the ground, unconscious. It felt like I was only out for one or two minutes, but a couple of people who saw me said that I was out for ten minutes. I'd had a second seizure. Somebody from the hotel recognized me from when we checked in the day before, so she called Kelly, who rushed down to the hotel lobby to find me on the ground.

Déjà vu! Paramedics, gurney, ambulance, emergency room! I was only in the emergency room for the day—I didn't have to stay overnight—but I knew, and Kelly knew, that this would be a major roadblock in my recovery progression. Once again, the seizure had affected my speech.

We were in Arizona for a week, but I couldn't have a good time because all I could think about was how to get my speech back. There was one upside, though—I had brought my flash cards along. I had a full set, from kindergarten through eighth grade, on a wide array of topics. Whenever Kelly drove us somewhere on that trip, I would ask her questions from the cards, like, "Who was Magellan?"

"No, I don't know that," she'd say.

I'd say, "I'm trying to connect questions and answers. This is the question. The answer is on the back." And I'd flip it over and read: "A Portuguese explorer who led the first expedition that sailed around the earth." Of course, I wouldn't remember all of that, but I would be quite pleased if I remembered he was an explorer.

Then, I'd go to the next one. After about an hour, I'd go back through the flash cards to see what I could remember. I found I couldn't recall any of them. More frustration.

Now, put yourself in Kelly's shoes: I couldn't talk. I didn't know much about Arizona before my stroke, and I was too preoccupied with rehabbing myself to focus on vacation planning, so Kelly had to do all of it.

She found a Native American reservation near Tucson for us to visit. We took a drive, two hours there and two hours back. That's when I really got into the flash cards.

"What animal eats meat? A lion or a rabbit?" I'd ask, and then, ignoring her answer, I'd read from the back of the card. "Lion."

"What sport did Michael Jordan play?" I'd ask. Then, I'd read the answer: "Basketball."

And so on. This went on for the first hour or so of our drive. It often took me several attempts to read the questions without errors. To Kelly's credit, she didn't get pissed, but she got more and more annoyed.

I included the flash cards in my weekly routine when we returned home from our vacation. I kept pushing myself harder. I started with five different cards every day and then jumped to ten. I had to rebuild my memory. I went from second- to third-grade vocabulary during that trip. Kelly was impressed with the determination and grit that I had (and still have) to go through those flash cards, always taking baby steps.

- - -

"I think I should ask the resort golf pro to see if he can help you learn to play," Kelly told me after I had had a little time to recover from the seizure. We were still in Scottsdale and seated right on a beautiful golf course.

I decided to follow her advice.

"Okay, Ted," the golf pro addressed me. "Let's see what you know." He placed a ball on the tee and handed me a club. I stepped up, lined up correctly, but everything else felt awkward. I could grip the club, pull it back a little, and move it forward through the ball, but the ball just dribbled off the tee. I didn't have any power; my legs and hips didn't move. I could walk, but I couldn't move my legs while trying to hit the ball. "That's okay. That's okay," he reassured me.

That's pathetic, I thought.

"You just have to rotate your hips at the waist," he said and showed me the motion, but I couldn't move my waist. While I was trying to figure out the clubs, the pro told Kelly I was like a first grader, but it would come. First comes the coordination.

This was one of those times I thought about giving up. I thought golf wouldn't work for me. I knew how to swing the club; I had been a baseball player all my life—I knew how to swing a bat. Now, after having a stroke, I couldn't do it.

I can't do this. What if the doctors are right? I'll never be able to play sports again. What about retirement, I thought in a panic. *I'll be bored to insanity. I have to be able to do something—golf, tennis, boating . . . something.* My mind raced. *I've got to choose one now, so I can do it later, when I retire.*

If I tried to do all three, at that point, I'd do a shit job at all of them.

It's got to be golf. I like golf. I was good at hitting the ball before. I can be good again. To hell with the doctors. I'll prove them wrong.

I decided I was through with Scottsdale, but I would play golf eventually. I would get better to prove to myself that there are things I can do, by focusing—stroke or no stroke.

Today, I can usually hit the ball 270 yards using my driver.

CHAPTER 16

Taking Charge Again

When we got back to Chicago from our vacation of sorts in Scottsdale, I returned to my regular routine: RIC in the city on Mondays and Wednesdays and Northwestern on Tuesdays and Thursdays. I worked out. I went for acupuncture. Once a week, I saw Sherrie for English as a Second Language at Loyola. I walked my dog. Once a week, I saw Doreen, my therapist. And, I saw a psychologist twice a week to help keep an even-keel attitude.

As a stroke survivor, there is a lot to contend with—the physical side, the mental aspects, the emotional effects of recovery, and even the way others interact with you. All of this is difficult to handle, which is why it is highly recommended that a psychiatrist or psychologist play a part in the rehabilitation.

"Ted, I found a psychiatrist for you. He works at RIC, so it'll be convenient," Kelly said while folding laundry one afternoon not too long after we'd returned from Scottsdale.

"Oh?" I asked, trying not to let the frustration ooze through.

"Yeah. I'll make an appointment for you," she said.

I didn't respond. I was too annoyed.

The RIC psychiatrist that Kelly found knew what had happened to me. But I didn't like Kelly saying that I should use this particular person. I'm too independent.

I'll make the decisions here. I don't like him. I'll decide when and who should be my psychiatrist, I thought.

Kelly didn't think I'd ever pick up the telephone to call a psychologist on my own. I waited two months or so, and then I did pick up the phone. I found a name by doing some research on my own: Dr. Leigh Chethik. He practiced private therapy three days a week, and the other two days he worked at RIC in the hospital, so it was a good fit. He knew about stroke and aphasia. He was perfect. When I first started seeing Dr. Chethik, he had trouble understanding me, but as time went by, that got much better.

- - -

Sometime in 2007 or 2008, I had dinner with my previous boss from Citadel. He wanted to see how I was doing and what activities I was involved in. By then, my comprehension wasn't 100 percent, but there had been significant improvement. I was talking in phrases and short colloquial sentences.

I needed some input from him.

"I need to figure out what I'm going to do now that I've been given this new life," I told him.

He nodded thoughtfully, and I went on. "I'm thinking about moving to Southern California."

"Really? When?" he responded. "It would certainly be a change of scenery. What will you do there?"

I shrugged. "Start over."

"Sounds like you have a plan, then." Although he didn't say it, I knew he was happy for me. The stroke hadn't taken me down. I had endured and worked as hard to rehab myself as I had for him.

We shook hands, and he left. Right then, I knew I'd made my decision. Staying in Chicago, seeing the financial district buildings that I had been accustomed to working in, seeing the hospital where

I basically lived for eight weeks after my stroke . . . no, none of this excited me.

Exercise Turns into Strategy

Meanwhile, in 2007, the people at RIC (the aphasia director and some stroke/aphasia doctors) wanted to know about my other aphasia program experiences. They knew I had gone to the experimental program in Orlando, but they were more interested in learning about the UMAP program. They wanted to know which program I felt had given me the most benefit.

"Which program had better experiments, therapists, settings, or techniques for you? How many participants attended? Could you help us set up the same thing at RIC? How would that look? Do you think you could put together a brief presentation for us?" they asked me.

Can I do this? I wondered. *I've given plenty of presentations in the past, but the stroke . . .* I didn't say anything aloud. I didn't give them a definitive answer, but I decided to do it. I started preparing without anyone knowing my plan. It was, in essence, a strategy development exercise to see if I could define and plan a strategy—in this case, develop a new, intensive aphasia program. I had learned how to formulate, create, and execute strategies thanks to my education from Wharton—it's where my roots were. I started by going back to UMAP, this time as a consultant, not as a patient. I stayed for two days, observing and taking notes.

Then, I toured the Adler Aphasia Center in Maywood, New Jersey. Their program was totally different from UMAP. Instead of being attached to a hospital or university, they had a stand-alone building totally dedicated to aphasia. It was strictly an outpatient facility.

Buses picked up the participants Monday through Thursday and brought them to a large building: thirty to forty people from the New York–New Jersey area on Mondays and Wednesdays and a different group on Tuesdays and Thursdays. The clinicians ran a different group every hour, and the facility also had a lounge with couches,

TVs, a small kitchen, tables, and computers that could be used during personal time. If someone didn't want to participate in a group, they had the option to spend time alone in the lounge, watching television or using the computer. There was even the option to attend a group here and there but still spend the whole day at the facility, doing other individual activities and socializing with other stroke survivors at lunch.

I segregated my day to be in groups in the morning and then the computer lab from one to three p.m. At four o'clock p.m., the buses came back and took everyone home. I stayed and talked to the director of the program about how they did it—how they made this program so enjoyable to be a part of. There were no patients at the facility on Fridays, just the therapists who planned their clients' activities for the next week.

I also toured the Aphasia Institute in Toronto, Ontario. Their program was like a combination of Adler and UMAP. They invited Toastmasters to come and present different topics and speaking guidelines, and then three or four stroke survivors would speak. Afterward, the instructors and Toastmasters would give critiques on what the people with aphasia struggled with. They gave tips on how to improve for next time. This was valuable information for survivors and caregivers.

When I came back from these three facilities, I had a proven model in my mind. If you wanted an aphasia program that could go on without a definite end date, so that you made it part of your daily living, then New Jersey's example would be the way to go. I could see that people who went to Adler used it as a new routine, like going to the club, attending group sessions to learn and improve and building that structure into their lives. If you wanted something more like a blast of intensive therapy for a short-term duration, and to build it as one of the components of your overall rehab plan, UMAP or Toronto was the answer.

I wrote up my conclusions and suggestions and brought them to Dr. Elliot Roth, RIC's medical director of patient recovery and professor at Northwestern Feinberg School of Medicine. I also presented to Leora Cherney, RIC's director of aphasia research and treatment.

"Look, why don't you expand this and give us a strategy for this new aphasia business? We would like to have something like this," Dr. Roth told me after seeing what I had prepared.

I couldn't believe it: They took my plan and ran with it. They kept the Aphasia Club, but they added a new program based on my strategy so patients could go through six weeks of intensive therapy, right there, at the Rehabilitation Institute of Chicago.

I learned a lot of valuable information from doing this exercise, especially how to relearn a lot of skills that I had before the stroke. I could still do that kind of strategic planning job, after I had experienced a massive stroke, while dealing with the aphasia. I could still formulate and write on a level that required the abilities and skills I had used throughout my career, especially those I had learned at Wharton. Albeit, my communication wasn't on the same level as it had been before my stroke, and I needed way more time to process things.

But, at least I was moving in the right direction. I found that incredibly reassuring. Two years after my stroke, my writing and speaking were a little better than they had been, and they were dependent on each other for improvement. I could see the light at the end of the tunnel—the day that both would work in concert. I was plugging away, and this project kept me positive and my emotions intact.

Tony

Right after Ted had his stroke, I read up on how it was supposed to affect him. That's when it really hit me. I realized he was in for a lot of challenges, and he might not ever be the same. He might get frustrated or angry because he has aphasia—he has this disability. He might get angry and ask himself, *Why me?*

Ted was totally the opposite. But that's Ted. The stroke did take some things away from him, but it did not take one of the biggest parts of him, which was his ability to rise to any challenge.

Now he's in this different environment. His challenge now, day to day, is staying ahead of the curve. That's why he's always busy.

One day, several years after his stroke, we were casually talking, and he was telling me about things he was doing, still totally involved with stroke research and aphasia, and he said, "Yeah, I did a speech at NYU."

"A what?"

"Oh yeah, I did a speech for a couple hundred people and talked to them about my stroke, aphasia, and stuff like that."

Whatever he's faced with, he just deals with it, he works on formulating the best form of attack. Nothing is going to stop him from continuing to be productive and successful. Staying busy motivates him.

That's so Ted.

CHAPTER 17

Expanding Creativity

I n the summer of 2007, Leora Cherney from RIC approached me and offered me the chance to participate in the Archeworks program in Chicago. Archeworks offers a one-year postgraduate program in public interest community design, change, and implementation. This was an opportunity to be immersed in a class with regular people, as opposed to being segregated into those with fellow stroke survivors. It would be a good barometer of whether I could progress while working with others.

Archeworks' learning philosophy fosters an approach of design thinking and enabling. There are about twenty students in the program every year, and they select from three public interest projects to work on.

When I went there in September 2007, the first of the three big projects they had going on at the time was one that dealt with a sustainable food cycle at a nature preserve. I didn't know (or want to know) what that was; I listened to the project overview and decided that it definitely wasn't for me.

The next was Engaging Chicago's International Communities. The hope with this project was that Chicago would be selected as the city to host the 2016 Olympics. The concept was to design a community for the Olympics in Chicago. I definitely wanted to be on that project, but I couldn't because of my stroke and because of the last project that was offered.

The last project was the Design of Products for Stroke Survivors for Improved Work and Home Life program. I had been offered the chance to enter in this Archeworks program with one other stroke survivor, and because RIC in the city had partnered with Archeworks, I would be a team member working on a project that focused solely on improving stroke survivors' daily lives. There were eight people, including me, that would work on the project and participate in the stroke-enabling initiative.

Being part of the Archeworks project was the equivalent of getting extra credit at the school, but not a requirement. Everybody who went through Archeworks had different reasons for participating. For example, it allowed young students to expand their social contacts and interactions, with the hopes of getting a better job. In my case, it was to progress my rehab to better my speech and overall communication. I also hoped to improve team skills while dealing with the challenge of having aphasia and contribute to designing new products or ideas to help stroke survivors.

Building a Stage through Teamwork

Before we started on the Archeworks project, a dozen of us did a unique pre-Archeworks project over the summer. This proved to be exciting and extremely challenging. We built a movable outdoor bandstand that stood eight feet high and approximately twenty feet in diameter. We had to build a cantilevered roof so the entire audience, who would be in a 180-degree arc around the stage, could see the performers. This was the goal: to design, build, and put the stage in action.

For me, participating in the project applied directly to my language challenges. I got out there and worked closely with the other team members and dealt with any problems or impediments as they came up. My aim was to be a project team member that didn't stop the team's progress for meeting the goal. I wanted to be an asset for the team. And that happened! The physical work was unlike anything I had done in more than twenty years, and I'd never built anything before in my life!

I suppose it would be like a carpenter being asked to assess the financial viability of a proposed investment. But the project was possibly even more awkward because I was still regaining the use of my right side. So, trying to hold and operate the drill or trying to hammer in the nails involved a steep learning curve. We were building a prefabricated structure in a warehouse to be moved to the site in Minnesota in pieces. And I had to get along with fourteen people. I didn't know any of them, including the instructor. They didn't know me, but they knew that I was a stroke survivor.

I faced the challenge of using my right hand, making new friends, and communicating effectively with a team, and then there was the actual problem solving.

"This, folks, is our project," the instructor said, placing a small model on the table and spinning it so we could see it from all angles. "We have to figure out how to build this, but on a much larger scale, of course. But first, let's start with this," he said, dumping a box of supplies in front of us. Slowly but surely, we were able to replicate the model.

The model taught us to leverage each other's strengths and to coordinate to build the model as a team. It was like when your parents gave you a model airplane with a thousand parts and you had to figure out how to put it together. This was right brain versus left brain stuff, and my left brain still wasn't strong at that point. My right side ultimately took over, which meant focusing on visual objects and logic.

"Well done," the instructor said as he spun our model and appreciated the construction, which had taken us three weeks. "Very well done! I guess this means we're ready for the real deal."

I had to push myself to go out to the workshop site, which was in a small town outside of the city, in an industrial lower-income neighborhood. I had to be there Monday to Friday, from eight a.m. to six p.m., building things using my hands and tools, and I was problem solving. I loved it. I thought, *Well, shit, maybe I should have gone into building houses before!*

After we completed building the stage, the instructor said, "It's time to move this thing to Minnesota and put it into action. The arts community will use it for performances."

So, we split the bandstand into logical components, loaded it into three vehicles, and headed off to Minnesota to set it up, which took two weeks to complete. It was a huge new stage for them. It was August, very sticky and hot, but I loved the physical and mental challenges.

Real Archeworks: Rediscovering Communication

After we came back from Minnesota, I started going to Archeworks in a warehouse-like facility near my townhouse in Chicago two or three evenings a week, from five to nine. I attended classes there, and I met the rest of my project team to start the actual project—a project to design innovative ways for stroke survivors to reintegrate into their daily lives. I also went back to the *ad infinitum* therapies at RIC in the city.

"Last year, the project team really focused on how we could physically improve the life of a person who just experienced a stroke," the instructor explained and then showed us a tray that could be used for multiple purposes. "Try lifting it," he said.

Each of us tried. It was awkward. The tray was not balanced for the average person. "As many of you know," he continued, "mundane tasks can be quite complicated for those who have suffered a stroke. By redistributing the weight of the tray, we can allow a stroke victim to carry the majority of the burden with the stronger side of their body." We all admired the tray and the concept before he set it aside and continued. "This year, we will focus on helping stroke survivors and caregivers discover different ways of doing their daily activities."

We met in the middle of Archeworks' warehouse-like building with a handful of instructors. Then, the three groups would separate, each moving to a different area of the huge room to work on their projects.

The first thing my project team did was talk about the ethics, morals, philosophies, and values of creating design in the public interest. We started our project by creating our strategic mission: "We are strongly committed to define aphasia by not only those with aphasia but also by those who are caregivers, family, and friends in the community. We are also committed to design solutions that will help educate and improve communication." We would be required to do four presentations over the course of the year in front of a hundred colleagues, staff, and instructors so they could see the progression of our work.

As part of our project, each of us worked with three or four stroke survivor outpatients from RIC in the city. I set up an hour to talk to them about what had happened to them, what kind of stroke they'd had, and what their life was like now. Then, I'd share with them my story and what Archeworks was all about. I'd also explain why I decided to participate.

They had caregivers with them, of course, and I could tell that they didn't want them there. They wanted to see if they could interact with another stroke survivor on their own. They felt they could make mistakes more comfortably because I was one of them. I had gone through the same thing. My team invited the stroke survivors to come to our presentations throughout the year, and two of the survivors in my group showed up, which was significant for me because I gained a rapport with these survivors. And they felt empowered because they could see my involvement in this project and that I, a stroke survivor, was able to relearn things and participate. I could collaborate with team members and develop presentations that I had to deliver to others without aphasia—which all played a part in my recovery and coming back into the community.

Starbucks

In the concept stage of the project, we were brainstorming different ideas and products, and I was quick to chime in.

"Starbucks," I blurted out one evening.

When the proclamation was met with questioning looks, I explained to the best of my abilities. Starbucks is a huge corporation that started with a simple cup of coffee and lattes. They now have myriad choices in drinks, foods, and other items. At Starbucks, you have to go into the coffee shop, up to the counter, and order. As most people know, many Starbucks menu items are hard to pronounce for the average person. People with aphasia want coffee too, but to communicate this, they have to express themselves in different ways. We needed to address this. It is already hard for the average person to order at Starbucks. Aphasia makes the process of ordering much more complicated.

My team and I created a prototype menu on a Starbucks cup sleeve so people with aphasia didn't have to talk to the barista to order. Instead, they could simply check what they wanted—a vanilla latte with skim milk, for instance—on the sleeve. It had the flavors, the size, and all the other information the barista would need. It was a different way to communicate.

I picked three Starbucks in Chicago that were in close proximity to my usual routes and went in to talk to the managers. For the first meeting, I went with two other people from my group. I had to describe what we were doing. The other two people let me do the talking to see if I could do it. The second and third Starbucks, I went to alone. One was near RIC in the city, and the other was in the middle of the financial district of Chicago. I collected information during the day, and I'd go back to my group at night to tell them what I'd learned. Gathering that information was my part of the project. I asked the managers of each shop questions like, "Are you familiar with terms like *stroke* and *aphasia*? Could you teach your employees what aphasia is and the impact of this disability on someone's daily life? What would your employees think about people with stroke and aphasia?" I added their comments to my final presentation.

As we ironed out the details, I found that I was the one being interviewed by the other members of the group.

"Will that work there? As a stroke survivor, if you went into

Coffee Menu Card

Coffeehouses continue to function as centers of communication. Please use this guide to order your coffee and promote aphasia awareness

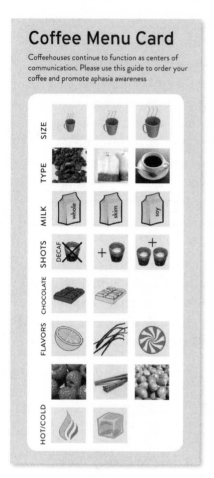

Starbucks and saw this flyer on the counter, would you pick it up and give it to the barista?" they asked me.

"Yeah, I would," I answered.

"Is the flyer enough? Should it just help with ordering or should it be an informational piece as well?"

In the end, we created a series of brochures that a Starbucks customer could carry with them. It had the same information as the sleeve, plus an explanation of stroke and aphasia—a loss of words, not a loss of intelligence—and some tips about communication. On the back, it listed aphasia and stroke community support centers (i.e., one featured local aphasia and stroke support facilities, and another featured national organizations). These brochures served as a communication tool—a way to get the message of aphasia out there so that people would know what the term meant.

- - -

I had to write a script for each of my four presentations, which was good because I knew if I didn't write it down, I would mess up and experience embarrassment. But the real challenge for me was to speak it out loud in front of the group without allowing my fear to show. I was anxious, and there was a lot of pressure to deliver this speech. I had done hundreds of presentations over the course of my career—more than I can possibly count. I had been persuasive enough to win over top competitors, to deliver our services to top-tier institutions. Those presentations enabled me to grow the Tokyo Price Waterhouse

Financial Services Consulting practice from nothing into a thriving business. For those four presentations at Archeworks, I couldn't even make eye contact with a hundred people in front of me because I had to read from my script for the entire fifteen-minute speech.

It's another challenge that I continually strive to overcome.

But looking back at the experience of participating in the Archeworks program, I realize that it helped me to improve my language, my presentation skills, and my ability to socialize with new friends. And more than that, I gained a great deal in myself: more self-confidence, self-esteem, a better understanding of what I need in my life, and courage. I became a more well-rounded individual.

CHAPTER 18

Sports as My Recovery

ooking back, I think the reason why I loved the stage project with Archeworks so much was because of the physical activity. I like to move, to challenge my body. When I was at the gym, I would watch people come in after me and leave before me. I was using standard barbells, cardio machines, and Smith machines, and I did things like crunches and squats. Even that wasn't enough. I liked how exercise impacted me physically, but I also found it had a positive effect on my speech recovery. So, I took on golf, Pilates, boxing, and eventually, yoga.

After my experience with the golf pro in Scottsdale, I had kept the idea of playing golf in the back of my mind. I had even called RIC to see if they offered any sort of golf program. In February of 2008, I learned that the head of the sports program at RIC in the city was Patrick Byrne. I thought, *This could be a new way to build new neural pathways to help my speech, plus make new friends, if I can get to the point where I can play.* And after a little more consideration, I called him directly.

"You're teaching stroke people to golf, right?" I asked him.

"Yeah, I'm doing it right now. I'm teaching people who have had strokes and people who have cerebral palsy and Parkinson's disease. What do you have?" he asked, in response.

"I experienced a stroke," I explained as well as I could. "Two years." My speech was slow, and I had to pause several times to try to find the right words to express myself. "I aphasia . . . ummm . . . hard . . . ummm . . . understand . . ." I apologized. He was patient, as I further explained that the right side of my body was paralyzed, and that I was trying to get my physical body to where it was before my stroke.

Patrick replied, "I understand enough. I think you should try this. We're practicing tomorrow night at the range near RIC in the city; come down, and I'll tell you if you can play or if you can't."

At the time, I was learning to formulate sentences, remembering idioms, and moving up from using simple phrases. I was getting into golf, and I needed another "dictionary" for my new golf vocabulary.

I met Patrick and the rest of the group the next night at the driving range. When I walked up to shake his hand, I marveled again at the fact that Patrick was the head of the sports program and a highly respected golfer, despite the fact that he had only one leg. *Wow . . . this is a guy who is calm. He lives a normal life and has a job as an instructor to teach people, with disabilities and without, to golf. Now that is an inspiration!*

When it was my turn to practice my swing, I swatted the ball and hit it. This time, my waist moved. I knew I could do this, because now I knew what the concepts *coordination* and *integration of my body* meant, and I could apply them. Before, I hadn't comprehended that my entire body had to move as one unit; it was something I'd been teaching myself. For a split second, I thought about my high school days, playing basketball, football, and baseball. *It's awful*, I thought. *The stroke took it all away. All those skills that I worked so hard to hone . . . they're all gone. Now I have to relearn all of it.* It was sad. I was depressed by the thought, but I had to get beyond it so I could play sports again.

After I swatted five balls, Patrick said, "You have to tell me where your stroke disability is coming from. You're hitting balls two hundred yards! It's not coming from your right side. So where is it?" I explained the left-brain versus right-brain concept and how I used to be right-handed and that I was working out four or five times a week. He smiled. "You will not have any problems hitting golf balls."

There were eight or nine other players. There was a guy with cerebral palsy, a guy with Parkinson's, and another guy who also had a stroke. The rest had other forms of disabilities. Not only were we dealing with physical deficiencies, but we were also contending with various levels of speech proficiency. Above all that, these were people who had a lot of emotional and psychological issues to deal with. That became clear quite quickly.

"All right, just a nice easy swing and follow-through," Patrick told one of the other players who was preparing to drive the ball. His swing was not overly smooth, and that meant that his drive didn't go too far. The guy stopped and slammed the club into the ground. Patrick had to calm him down.

I wasn't invincible to troubles on the course, by any means.

"We'll let you take a turn driving the cart today," Patrick told me at the start of one round. He handed me the key and told me to follow him. He jumped in another cart and started down the path. I had to press a lever to make it go in reverse. Before my stroke I knew that, but now I didn't remember. I messed it up. I couldn't remember how to go back. So, my foot pressed the accelerator, and I hit the back of Patrick's cart.

"It's going to happen to anybody with a disability," Patrick said, but I was really sorry that I had made that mistake. Luckily, I had become good friends with Patrick by then.

I realized, through golf, that getting my coordination back would also provide a new way of retraining my brain. The physical trainers had always told me, "It's all about muscle memory. If you do it so many times, it'll become automatic." I worked out every day. One day, while I was working out at Crunch Fitness, a light came on in my head: *I can do this every day if I exercise my physical body. That's what's going to help my brain. You watch.*

During this time, Kelly was checking my progress. She noted that when I went to the gym, where I'd run—I started at fifteen minutes on the treadmill and worked up to thirty minutes—I'd come home tired, but my speech got better. The change was quite noticeable. She called my neurologist and my doctor and told them.

One day, arriving at the gym a little earlier than usual, I noticed that a different sort of class was taking place in the aerobics studio. I stayed to watch for a few minutes.

What is this? I thought as I watched the participants stretch and exercise only their legs with precise control. *I have to try this.* It involved such concentration that I knew, immediately, it would be good for me. I liked the idea of Pilates more than yoga because yoga, which was offered to me, was more spiritual and meditative than physical. I liked the physical aspect. I believed that it could help me build those new neurons, new synaptic pathways in my brain. When I went to the Pilates class for the first time, I was quiet. I had to listen to what the instructors said in order to comprehend it and execute what I heard.

What would have been considered simple to someone else was much more difficult for me. I became quite visual. The Pilates training made me work on finding new ways to execute simple tasks, which made it a tough but beneficial year.

Kelly

He did Pilates for a while.

Then he said, "I don't know if that's making a difference anymore. Now I'm going to try boxing."

And that helped his speech, just as Pilates had at first.

"Now I'm going to try acupuncture," he said.

When things didn't work out for Ted, he would say, "Okay, I shouldn't have done it that way. Fix it. Let's move on."

He has an unbelievable resiliency for moving forward.

— — —

Pilates was good, but it wasn't as great as I wanted it to be. I was looking for something else. So, when I saw the story about a boxer who experienced a stroke and came back from it and was able to get back into the ring again, I was inspired. He played actual matches!

He didn't care if he won or lost—it was simply about getting into the ring again. At the time, I was working with a trainer at Crunch Fitness in Chicago, so I asked him, "Do you do boxing here? Can you teach me the basics?"

"Yes. That's a good cardio for you, and it takes a lot of coordination."

I began learning to box almost immediately. I would jab with my left hand and then land a cross with my right. I switched to jab with the right and cross with the left, the same as a southpaw boxer. It made me use both sides of my brain in a new way. I had to use my four limbs, like in golf, but it took a different kind of coordination—and that effort helped my brain heal, which also meant improved speech. It was like when, earlier in the recovery, I alternated which hand I used to shave. It was all about mastering control over both sides of my body.

Pushing My Brain

Throughout all of it—recovery, boxing, and exercising in general—I was slowly regaining full use of my right side instead of only being able to use my left side. There was a very visual aspect to my recovery. If I could see somebody do something, then I could follow it and mimic what they did. It's hard to explain how my brain worked after the stroke. If I was told to make the bed, I would just see a messy bed but not know how to make the right movements to make it. If, though, I could visualize someone making the bed in my mind, then my brain could make the connection between the words and the actions. I had to adapt to this new way of doing things.

All those years before my stroke, I was logical, practical, task, and function oriented. I had to do this, this, and this. I had to call this person, that person, and so on. I kept a mental list for everything.

That's the way I always thought. I had a task list, a project plan. Always.

But now, I couldn't remember a plan. I couldn't keep a list in my head. But I wanted my mind, my brain, to get to the results. I didn't want to have any stops with my speech when I got into a conversation. I had to grasp ideas in a different way, and I had to use simple words to convey ideas. This process of changing my thought patterns was not easy.

I had to keep prioritized task lists and calendars as I had done before my stroke, but I also had to work hard to strengthen my short-term memory. I had to focus on visualization—picturing the task, the actions needed to perform that task, and the intended result. I had to group the tasks that I wanted or needed to complete throughout the day. I thought of this as breaking the list down into chunks, and it worked.

I was speaking more spontaneously, more off-the-cuff. I was learning to use both the analytical and creative sides of my brain. Once I got past the frustration and anxiety, I found that I enjoyed a new way of seeing things. It opened me up to new experiences and widened my perspective. This ability to use different facets of my brain, which I had concentrated on developing during my rehab, gave me another set of tools to play with. It provided me tools I needed to communicate more effectively.

CHAPTER 19

Life Changes

was doing well not only with my various therapies but also with getting out into the world and doing new activities.

- I went through the Archeworks program—check.

- I developed a model strategy for starting up a new aphasia center—check.

- I kept in contact with the aphasia centers that I had attended or worked with and had met the top therapists at each of them—check.

- The National Aphasia Institute asked me to serve on their advisory board—check.

I walked my dog twice a day—mornings and evenings—and played with him before I went to bed. I worked out. I boxed. I hit golf balls. I went to all my various therapies. I joined and participated in the RIC disability golf club. I was gaining ground every day. I had built good relationships with the therapists and clinicians.

But there wasn't a stable or ongoing initiative for me that I could sink my teeth into. I was always thinking, *What am I going to do now? Should I leverage some of my abilities that I learned during the rehab process into one of the aphasia center's initiatives? Volunteer? Leverage my contacts? Location? Keep doing more of the same?* I needed more excitement.

By then, Kelly was going to Northeastern Illinois University to study social work and was working hard to establish a career path for herself. She wanted an identity separate from mine, and I couldn't blame her. I had been single-minded about my career all those years, and then I was equally single-minded about my recovery. And by now, we already had a strong feeling that divorce was on the horizon.

I wanted a clean slate, a fresh perspective. Every time I saw the Chicago or New York City skyline, I thought about my former life in finance. I thought about going back to New York, where I grew up and started my career. I thought about who I used to be and who I was now.

That's going to kill me, just to see Chicago or New York from the plane. It's always going to remind me of going back, I often thought. Those skylines were a constant reminder of the financial world I wasn't part of anymore. They were everything I'd lost.

Some people who retire from Chicago or New York move to Florida. I didn't want retirement living. I wanted a new life—new friends, new activities, new ways of giving back to the community. Southern California kept coming to mind.

I was still seeing my psychologist, Leigh, to talk about the feelings and experiences after having a stroke: growing apart from friends, facing divorce, and especially figuring out, dealing with, and navigating through aphasia. I had a great connection with Leigh. It was sometimes difficult to get my ideas across because of my speech, but he understood. He provided me much-needed support as I made important decisions.

In 2009, I said to Leigh, "Kelly and I were discussing a separation before I had the stroke, and my bet is Kelly and I will probably get a divorce. How do you think we should approach this?" I explained to him that our marriage was deteriorating.

"Go to a marriage counselor. I can help you talk through your end of it, but you need to do this together," he told me. "A counselor can help you work through things, help you decide if there is room for reconciliation."

He gave me the names of three psychologists who specialized in marriage and divorce.

"When you see each of these," he said, "make sure you and Kelly go together."

I was expecting to have some good conversations with Kelly so we would choose the right one together. So I broached the subject one evening.

"I've already found a counselor. I've been seeing him for about a month," she told me.

I sat down. I stood up. I sat down in the chair again and propped my head on my hands. I stared at her. As her words sank in, anger flooded me. Actually, that's putting it mildly. There was steam coming from my ears.

"We go together. Marriage counseling!" I yelled.

"I had to talk to someone, Ted. This isn't working."

"Together!" I snapped again.

"You can come next time," she answered with a shrug and a scowl. I went, but I just kept thinking that she'd already swayed the counselor, that she'd started the process without me.

But in all fairness, we had talked about ending our marriage before I had my stroke. She had stood by me for four and a half years while I fought to recover even though our marriage hadn't been particularly strong beforehand. Now, we both knew I was strong enough to handle life on my own, so we saw the marriage counselor once a week over the next four or five months, mostly to identify our irreconcilable differences, recognize them, and eventually, to get a divorce.

"Thinking about moving to California," I said in one session with Leigh.

"Oh yeah? The vacation house?" he asked, because I had already told him that Kelly and I were talking about getting a second house out there.

"By myself," I answered, shaking my head. "No vacation. Divorce."

"You have to understand that you won't know anybody there."

I wanted to have a house in Newport Beach, in Southern California. "Do you think I can start a new, happy life there?" I asked.

"Yeah . . . eventually," he said.

We discussed the fact that I would be sad and depressed due to the divorce. It would feel like I was truly alone and nothing was left. He was sorry about my divorce. "But you'll bounce back," he said.

In October, Kelly helped me buy a new house in Newport Beach and took care of most of the furnishings for it. I didn't know what types of rugs would go with the sofa, what sort of chairs would fit in the space, what colors would work on my walls, and so on. I could have done this mostly myself, but it would have been a slow process as a stroke survivor with aphasia challenges.

--- --- ---

The lawyer stuff started in November 2009. We were amenable about it, although we both got emotional, as would be expected. At first, before my stroke, I didn't want the divorce, but we had grown so far apart that it made the most sense for both of us. I came to terms with it after a lot of soul searching. Now that she was getting her degree, we both needed to live our own lives, separate from each other.

Kelly

The furniture was all ordered by the time we filed for divorce, but it wasn't in, so he was still living at our place in Chicago. At the beginning of 2010, once the furniture started to arrive, he moved to California.

I flew out there to help him settle in that January, and we went to a Lakers game. He asked me to stay on, to help him with some of the stuff, so I did.

We're still good friends. We don't talk about our current relationships—nothing like that—but I'm probably one of the first people he tells about what he's doing with therapy, who he's speaking to about his rehab, and about this book. We still talk on a somewhat regular basis. He will always be a dear friend.

CHAPTER 20

Fresh House, Fresh Start, and Socialization

I officially moved to California on January 1, 2010.

I knew there were things about setting up the new house that I couldn't and didn't want to deal with, so Kelly came to California with an interior designer from Chicago. For instance, the color of my living room walls was a detail I didn't need to worry about. That's what the interior designer was for. Kelly was in town for five days, and the decorator was there for three days. Kelly wanted me to have a say in the colors and patterns for the space, and she'd call me over to get my views on colors, but I didn't even know what a window treatment was because of the aphasia challenges—memory and vocabulary were still an issue. My bigger concern was getting the furniture in the house.

I wanted a TV. I wanted the same kind of home entertainment center I had in Chicago. I knew there had to be a way to buy a TV, put it in my house, and fix the controls so I could program what to watch, but I wasn't at the point in my recovery where I could do it myself yet. I didn't know what to do.

So, I kept my eyes open for someone who could help with the

entertainment system situation while I searched out a psychologist. I knew that having that level of support would be essential, certainly more important than the entertainment center setup.

There was still a lot to contend with mentally and emotionally, because of the stroke, the divorce, the move, and all of the changes in my life that resulted. Ironically, it was around the same time that I found a psychologist that I felt comfortable with when I noticed an audio visual (AV) store across from Starbucks, which I walked to often to get a latte. I went in to see the AV specialist who owned the store, Tim Miner. When I told him what I wanted, he was curious about what had happened to me.

As I approached Tim that first time, I was worried and already rehearsing what I wanted to say in my head. I wanted to be sure that I could get my point across, that he would understand what I wanted. "I want a TV . . . an entertainment . . . the whole thing, set up."

"Do you mind if I ask you what's going on with your speech?" he asked.

"Stroke. Aphasia," I answered.

I was never ashamed, but that was a big moment for me. I knew I couldn't speak with the fluency I had before my stroke. I wasn't there yet; I wasn't ready. But I had to do something to help make my surroundings at home more comfortable.

I braced myself and managed to get into a conversation that lasted fifty, maybe sixty minutes. Ultimately, I knew that it was best to get more than one bid, so I visited two other AV stores as well and had AV specialists from all three come to my house to propose a bid.

I decided I wanted to work with Tim. He was a real person. He was likeable and was always understanding of—and fascinated by—my stroke. When choosing service providers, I considered if they were likeable or not and whether I could get along with them. I needed someone who would be patient with me and who knew what aphasia was. That had to come first, as simple as it sounds, before I considered his tech abilities, other customers' comments about his performance, price, and so on.

I knew he couldn't just pop in, put up a TV, and that would be that. He had to wire the whole place. But even before that, the mantle above the fireplace where I wanted the television to go had to be lowered. He had to get people to come to my home to fix that first. All in all, this became a large project, and I was dealing with three different people with three different skills. In the end, all the equipment was hidden in a coat closet, and I could control the whole thing from my iPad, including the sound on the patio. It worked great.

I built a friendly relationship with Tim as he and his team worked. One day, he said, "By the way, do you know what you're going to do with the walls?"

"What do you mean? I'm not going to break down the walls," I said.

"What pictures are you going to put up?" he asked, looking around, inspecting the space.

I had no idea. "I don't know anything about art."

Tim then told me about Peter Blake who lived in Laguna Beach, which was a short ride from my new home in Newport Beach. Peter owned and ran a fantastic contemporary art gallery. I met him, and we became great friends. He is from Hempstead, Long Island, New York. I really liked the art that he had in his gallery—the colors, the shapes, and the aesthetics. He gave me some pointers on contemporary art, and he introduced me to a few artists from Los Angeles and Orange County. It was through Peter that I began to delve in to the world of art; I had never given it much thought before my stroke.

There is a connection between people who have experienced a stroke and art. And without having ever heard of art therapy, I figured I would try it and enjoy it. This was a totally new and different way of enjoying life. I was hungry for new activities and enjoyed immersing myself into a new world. I found out later, after speaking to some of the doctors from UCI, that art therapy enriches people's lives through active art-making, like painting or sculpting, or collecting and experiencing art pieces, or going to see art in galleries or museums. Art therapy can help reduce stress, improve self-esteem and emotional health, and lower depression. Art became a source of joy and fulfillment in my life.

Eventually, I bought some pieces from Peter and learned a real appreciation for contemporary art. In early 2011, Peter called a member of the board of trustees for the Laguna Art Museum and recommended that I be considered to join the board. He told them I was smart and liked art and was exactly what they needed—I had a fresh perspective.

His recommendation held significant weight. I was contacted by one of the trustees and had a meeting with three members of the board to explain what Laguna Art Museum was and what being on the board meant for me. Not long after, I joined the board. This gave me a new and different avenue to learn about art—participating on a nonprofit board, giving my views on different museum-related issues, and socializing with people who shared my appreciation of art. I could get into art-related conversations with people, which would help me become comfortable with art terminology, and I would start having fun.

This constant conversational practice continued my recovery and withered away my aphasia every day. I had decided that if I picked one or two topics—like contemporary art—and learned about them, got comfortable with those subjects, and could have a deep conversation about them, the aphasia would lose its power in my life. Eventually, I would forget about it. It would no longer be a topic for my everyday conversations. My focus would be the actual topic—contemporary art.

This is not to say that serving on the board of an art museum in a new town, meeting and socializing with new colleagues, new patrons, and living with aphasia were easy. The members of the board were friendly, cordial, collegial, and serious when dealing with business issues, events, or initiatives. All in all, it was a group of extremely smart, some retired, and working executives from various aspects of their careers, and it was fun to interact with them as a member of the same board. Part of being a member of the board was trying to raise funds, encouraging people to donate, especially those from Orange

County. That was one area I couldn't help with. I didn't know anybody; I was still new as far as Orange County was concerned.

Instead, they put me in a subcommittee. When the executive director resigned at Laguna Art Museum, our committee was tasked with hiring the replacement. I researched the resumes for the potential directors selected by the subcommittee. I had to go out and talk to three potentials then go back to the next board meeting and summarize my views and impressions. I had to understand what people were saying—listen and comprehend. The actual job was easy for me, since I had been through this process a million times before in the financial world. But being an art museum trustee in a nonprofit institution was a little new for me, so I had to brush up on the related terms.

The socialization was a good fit for me, and I served on the board at the museum for three years. I took the initiative to meet as many people as I could. Tim, Peter, and the museum all helped me get out in the world and socialize. Peter introduced me to his girlfriend (who later became his wife). She had had a stroke also, and she too had found a deep love for art. She knew firsthand the frustrations, anxieties, and challenges of having aphasia, especially in a social setting, so we could speak with a level of understanding that others didn't share. All these relationships led to others, and because of all of that, I knew the relocation to California could work. I could meet new people and build relationships, but I still had questions. *What's my purpose? I had a stroke and I have aphasia, but can I help others? And if yes, then how?* I didn't know if helping people was a viable opportunity for me to pursue.

That's how my life in California grew. I was pursuing a different life than I had in New York and Chicago. I was learning new things that I hadn't been exposed to before. Before my stroke, I never would have done any of these things. There hadn't been time to appreciate art when I'd been jet-setting. But I loved how life on the West Coast was coming together. *I'm doing it on my own, my own terms*, I thought in those moments of excitement. Without my wife, without any therapists or psychologists to guide me, I built a new circle of friends and acquaintances. And regarding my recovery—well, that continued without me realizing it.

PART 4

-

Giving Back

CHAPTER 21

Therapy and Volunteering in Southern California

W hen I was still living in Chicago in 2008, I had sat down with Belma Hadziselimovic, the director of aphasia at Northwestern.

"Suppose I move to Southern California; what do you think about that?" I asked.

"That would be fine," she said after a moment.

"Could I do something like the therapy we do here out there?"

"Yes. There are programs on the West Coast."

"Where?" I asked.

"San Diego. It's near where you're going to live, a little over an hour away. When you go out there next, let me know. I'll call and let them know you're coming over to see what they have," she told me.

So, I did.

There was a clinic and research center with a program similar to Northwestern's called Speech, Language, and Hearing at San Diego State University (SDSU). I started working with them shortly after I moved. Twice a week, I'd spend mornings getting therapy from students or clinicians who were training to be therapists. Each semester,

I picked a book, and the clinician and I would read it at the same time. Then, we got into questions and answers about the book. When I got frustrated, I would think back.

I wouldn't have been able to read this two years ago. I wouldn't have understood it as well a year ago, I'd remind myself, to change the frustration into a calm, content state, recalling how well I was progressing.

I talked to the director at SDSU, and we agreed that I could do specific things with the clinicians. These things included memory tasks and working with tough vocabulary and idioms. The director also asked me to help her evaluate a group of students who practiced their therapy skills with adult stroke survivors. In addition, I did presentations for a number of courses that the students were taking as part of the speech programs.

Then, in the afternoon, I went to a different division of the speech, stroke, and aphasia area, which focused on aphasia research. I would do different experiments. The research analysts would ask me if I thought that particular exercise or experiment would work with aphasia patients, depending on how long ago they'd experienced their stroke.

At the same time that I was doing this work with SDSU research team, I had investigated volunteering at University of California, Irvine (UCI). When I called UCI to learn more about volunteering opportunities, I learned that they had a huge program dedicated to just that.

So, I attended the orientation and got a hands-on look at what would be involved. Afterward, I hung around so I could speak with the director of volunteering. I had questions to ask, questions about stroke, aphasia, neurology, and so on. She didn't have much time to speak that day, but she did tell me she would contact me later. Nevertheless, I was surprised when the call came through. She wanted to tell me more, because the UCI hospital had a lot to be proud of in the neurology department, including five or six doctors devoted to stroke prevention and treatment. Furthermore, she thought there might be specific volunteer tasks that would appeal to me, given my experiences.

She was right, and I was frequently at the hospital in UCI in the rooms with recent stroke victims, compiling stroke patient records, participating in stroke recovery groups to share my story, or doing rounds with doctors as they visited the rooms of people newly diagnosed with stroke.

I was at the UCI hospital when one of the stroke doctors introduced me to Steve Small. When I met him, I found that he was quite familiar to me. He was a world-renowned aphasia expert who had been doing research at the University of Chicago. He had worked with my experiments, evaluations, and research after I had my stroke in Chicago, but at that point, my brain was still fuzzy and my memory capabilities weren't there. When my stroke doctor from UCI introduced us, Dr. Small said he had heard the name Ted Baxter and knew I'd had a massive stroke. After meeting him, I called Kelly.

"Yes, I remember him," she said, surprising me. "You met him at the hospital at the University of Chicago, too, but you probably wouldn't remember that." She was right. I had been amazed at my name being recognized as a stroke patient. *Once upon a time, I was known in the financial industry as the go-to guy whether I was working at Price Waterhouse Consultants or whether I was working at CSFB or Citadel. Now, I'm known for something so very different.*

Coincidentally, Dr. Small had moved to California about six months after I did. He had taken a new job in neurology at the hospital at University of California, Irvine, and was building a new facility on neural brain recovery, including programs for stroke survivors. He wanted to pick my brain about strokes, aphasia, and the treatments that were offered in Southern California.

"Look, you want to join me? We'd love to have you because of your experience with stroke and rehabbing yourself. To be where you are now, compared to where you were after you had a stroke, it's remarkable. And that's great for us at University of California, Irvine," he said.

He went on. "I'm going to build a neural repair brain facility at UCI. I want you to work with therapists there and try our experiments. Our therapists are like researchers, like SDSU. They develop new methods by giving you written exercises, speech scripts to be read aloud, or selecting visual options on a computer. You will tell us if the experiments will work for stroke survivors.

"I know all your cadre of therapists in San Diego and Chicago. They probably don't even know I'm here in California. When you go there next time, tell them that I'm here and that you're going to help me with this," he told me.

And, like that, from what I'd learned through my experience, I was helping stroke doctors and neurologists at UCI and SDSU.

In May 2011, UCI campus had their annual stroke survivors' picnic, so I went. I figured it would be a good way to meet new stroke survivors, therapists, and doctors and learn about new health-related institutions. I walked around and met people, since I'd been to the hospital before but not the college campus.

The picnic allowed for a lot of socialization, and I came across someone who worked for the American Heart and Stroke Association and was responsible for the Western States region of running a golf clinic focused solely on stroke survivors. They usually run an annual golf clinic for stroke survivors in various locations—from Northern and Southern California to Arizona to Las Vegas—and they didn't have support to run that year's Orange County clinic. This fact came up during our conversation. Being a stroke survivor and having taken an interest in golf, I wanted to help. I found myself making introductions. I talked to a golf director from a golf club in Fullerton, California, and I told him about the program and asked if he would host the clinic. He agreed. At that moment, it was clear that I had made the right decision in attending that picnic—the golf clinic was able to happen in Orange County.

As I continued my walk around the picnic, I went over to the St. Jude's Hospital table and met their aphasia director, Candace Vickers. She couldn't believe I'd had a stroke.

"You're very intelligent with the stuff going on in your brain," she said at one point, and then introduced me to her husband, Terry, who had also had a stroke. We got to talking, and then she said,

"Ted, I run a communication recovery group program every Monday in a church in Fullerton. The church donated the space for students, clinicians, and aphasia-related clients, to give them a place to practice their speech, therapy techniques, and get used to interacting with other people with aphasia in a social setting. It provides the chance for people with aphasia—and caregivers—to converse and to do therapy one-on-one or as a group. This is totally volunteer based and overseen by St. Jude's Hospital. Why don't you come and just see? You don't have to be part of it. Obviously, you're out of the patient stage, but you could be a volunteer, an advocate for stroke and aphasia. You have a lot of strategies and tips that the other clinicians could learn from. And our clientele would really like you to socialize with them and learn from you in a different way."

Again, I had fallen into something wonderful, a relationship with St. Jude's Communication Recovery Group. There are many benefits that come with the role of volunteer clinician or an aphasia ambassador: I share my views with the other clinicians about their techniques and what they should and shouldn't do as a client; I work with the aphasia director to help organize and develop the stroke-survivor program; I get to practice my own speech; I help lead various groups of clients with different clinicians during the Monday mornings; and best of all, I go to universities and hospitals to present my story— what I had experienced, how I rehabbed myself, how it changed my life for the better, and what it took to get my life back. I was able to give stroke survivors and caregivers hope. Sometimes, I couldn't believe how far I'd come.

So Many Treatment Options!

"When are you going to write your book?"

I looked up at the question. It wasn't the first time I had been asked. The director of the aphasia program in San Diego looked directly at me, making it clear that it was a genuine question.

"I'll give it some thought. I'm not really the kind of guy who can just sit in my house, open my computer, and write." I shrugged. "I'm much better at being active, talking with people."

I wanted to make personal connections. I don't remember what was said next. I only remember thinking, *I could be a motivational speaker. I can tell audiences what it is like to experience a massive stroke and walk them through it from A to Z. I'm almost doing that now.*

I knew there was no single answer to recovering from stroke or aphasia, for that matter. No one has the panacea for treating, recovering from, or conquering this. I wanted to tell people, "This is the way I did it. This is what I didn't do, and this is all the stuff I did. And you know what? You can do things you didn't think you could ever do again after your stroke. It's called determination, will, focus, resiliency, and perseverance." As my thoughts followed this path, it got me thinking about all the things I hadn't tried.

I knew if I could have fit the things I didn't do into my routine, I would have. I didn't have time to practice singing, for example. When I lived in Chicago, my good friend Barry, who had a stroke similar to mine, went to a teacher who taught Jewish songs, and he asked me to come with him. But I didn't have the time. My schedule was full already. I chose sports, the gym, getting private therapy, going to RIC in the city, RIC in Northbrook, and Northwestern, and going to English classes. There was no time left for singing lessons.

I didn't try the hyperbaric chamber when I was in Chicago, either. A hyperbaric chamber is a large chamber in which the oxygen pressure is above normal for the atmosphere: It allows an individual to breathe in 100 percent pure oxygen. It has been a successful way for individuals to experience relief from decompression sickness, a hazard for scuba diving. It's also used to treat some medical conditions.

I had talked to Kelly about it, and we both thought it would be a good thing for me to do. She called my neurologist in Chicago.

"Ted would like to try the hyperbaric chamber," she explained. There was a moment of consideration.

"Let's see next time he comes in for a checkup visit," my neurologist responded.

Before that next meeting, I read an article in a journal about a woman who was a caregiver for her husband, and she started him on the hyperbaric chamber. I was taken aback by the time commitment, especially when I tried to figure out how I would fit it in with what I was already doing. I'd have to be in there five times a week for six to eight weeks so my system got used to breathing that much oxygen. It's supposed to help recovery in your brain cells.

I was already feeling hesitant because of what I had read—it was unproven—and when I met with the neurologist, he voiced concerns as well.

"Ted, I think it might be a bit late in the recovery for this, anyway. There really isn't any evidence to suggest that it would help in a case like yours, especially so long after the stroke." He sat for a moment, perhaps expecting me to argue for it. "If you had another seizure in the chamber . . . ," he started, and shook his head, "I don't think it is worth the risk." I agreed.

I didn't try yoga or meditation right away, either. It was too much inner focus, which made me uncomfortable in the first few years after my stroke, so I found different types of exercises. In time, though, my impressions of yoga changed, too. I calmed down after moving to California and starting my new life. Yoga and meditation now helps keep me grounded and my life balanced.

Part of my reason for communicating with other stroke survivors was to present them with all the possible alternatives that they could consider through their own recovery process. I recognize that although I had opted away from some of the recovery options, others could potentially benefit from them. I had to keep my mind open and give information rather than trying to sway others to take the same approach that I had. Because discovering the best approach that fit my needs was what worked for me, so it could work for others as well.

CHAPTER 22

Hello, Positive

"I don't really know what to do with myself," I said to my therapist in Orange County, not long after the UCI picnic events.

"It seems to me, Ted, that you have a lot on your plate."

I shrugged. "Yeah, I guess. It just feels like something is missing. There are a lot of things that I am doing right now, but I don't have a career anymore . . . And I don't have to work as hard on the recovery process now . . ."

"Give it some time, Ted. You've already done a lot" was the response. But I was getting impatient again. I was somewhat bored. I needed something exciting. I realized I was entering uncharted territory here.

I came across self-improvement mogul Tony Robbins not long after that conversation with my therapist, so I signed up for his "Unleash the Power Within" seminar in February 2013. It started me on the path to figuring out who I was, who I wanted to become, and what my purpose was.

"Life is a gift," Robbins said, "and it offers us the privilege, opportunity, and responsibility to give something back by becoming more." I was one among six thousand people who attended the event that long weekend, at the Los Angeles Convention Center. I started to realize that by doing more for others, I'd be happier with myself.

I don't know how the other attendees felt, but it was a life-altering event for me. Robbins was a dynamo. I was there, in front of the convention building, and I didn't know a soul there. After the first day, at one thirty a.m., getting ready to walk over fiery coals, he taught us how to change our mindsets and take mind over matter. "Overcome the unconscious fears that are holding you back," Robbins proclaims. "Storm across a bed of hot coals. Once you start doing what you thought was impossible, you'll conquer the other fires of your life with ease."

"Only those," he reminded us, "who have learned the power of sincere and selfless contribution will experience life's deeper joy, true fulfillment."

It was a message that would stand out for me, even though I had attended the conference only in the hopes to improve my delivery of presenting speeches and learn how to convey my story and my views regarding determination to my audience. He gave me that too, but that was the figurative cherry on top of something even better.

He had us sit down and think about what we had in our lives. "Write the list in order of priority," he said. And even though he was standing in front of a huge auditorium filled with people, I felt like he was speaking directly to me. I believed he could see in my face what I was slowly coming to realize. *My priorities were wrong before this stroke.* I wrote it down:

1. Work
2. Work
3. Work
4. Working out/Sports
5. Wife and Family

No wonder I ended up getting a divorce, I thought as I looked at the list. My career had been so important to me that my family and my wife had barely made the list.

Robbins said our first priority had to be physical body and health. If you don't have that, nothing else matters.

Our second priority should be our relationships. I broke my new-found priorities into three baskets:

1. To improve my relationships with my family—my brothers and sister and my close friends
2. To foster new and old friendships
3. To find someone to share my renewed life with

I made my fourth priority about education because I knew I had to improve my speech fluency and expand my word-finding skills. I learned the medical terms related to stroke, including aphasia, traumatic brain injury (TBI), left neglect, and others. I wanted to continue to learn about contemporary art and French wine.

My fifth priority was to do more small-scale public speaking. I could get out there to the hospitals and universities and tell audiences my story, share the determination, resolve, tenacity, and motivation. I wanted to build an Internet site and communication channels (social media) even if I didn't know exactly what it was going to be for, and I realized I wanted to write a book. And that led to the sixth goal on my list—giving back.

Though I had been pretty resistant to the idea of writing a book about my experiences, I sat there listening to Robbins and thought, *I need to give back. I can do that with this book, just as I can with the volunteer work.*

I realized that weekend that I have a purpose, a gift to deliver: telling people, especially the population living with disabilities, not to give up. That's a powerful message from a person who has been there, who is still in the stages of recovery, but who had turned the disability volume down and found a way to rebuild his life.

There were other ways that I could give back as well. I have now been involved with three hospitals. I give back all that I learned from my own life: therapy options, techniques, tips. I am an advocate for stroke and aphasia recovery. I have been on the board of trustees for three nonprofit institutions and continue to serve on one of them. I decided to give a donation to the Laguna College of Art and Design. They used my donation to focus on helping disabled students, and that was extremely gratifying. It felt good that I made a contribution that could change someone's life for the better.

"For those of you not yet retired, your occupation will be a priority," Robbins said. My occupation now is doing volunteer work, being a part of institutions' boards, and involving myself in philanthropic issues that will allow me to make a difference.

It was also about having time with myself—me time—to feel grateful to be alive and doing new things. I was done spending my days drinking coffee at Starbucks. I gave my second pug—the one I got when I moved to California—away to a good new home because I was using the pup as an excuse to not play golf, take trips, go to wine tastings, or meet new people. I really liked having a dog, but it was for the wrong reasons, and it was not the right time. It wasn't right for the pug, either. And I needed time to myself to regroup and ensure that I had my priorities straight.

I wrote down *travel*. Then, I added *NYC apartment* and *significant relationship*. Travel would be enjoyable, educational. The apartment would allow me to spend more time with my family. And significant relationship could lead to having a wife (and it did!).

Nancy

He's so much more fun now, laughing and smiling and joking—really knee-slapping—and having a good time. He was here for Christmas dinner with us. It was so awesome. He spent the whole day with us. He just jokes all the time now. You can sit there and make him laugh for hours. He's more lighthearted.

He always had a good time, but he used to be more serious. I didn't ever see him slap his knee in a conversation and get hysterical talking about something silly. And talking to him just about his life, what he does nowadays . . . It's refreshing . . . It's like he has a new life, and he will tell you that. It's so funny to watch.

— — —

"Don't worry. Why do you have to worry about this if it's in the future? The future's going to be what you want to make of it. Just live your life at the moment," Robbins said.

That spoke directly to me. I often wondered whether my life would always be centered around my stroke and aphasia. Would I ever be about something else? I used to be all about work and career. Now, I wanted my life to be more than only one thing. I was determined to be more. And if my decisions or path were a little off, I'd change or tweak it until I liked the path I was on.

I used to be so focused, so determined, so competitive that I wouldn't even let my little sister win a single game of Monopoly when we were kids. Now, I started thinking about how much she meant to me in my life, how much all my family meant, and how much happiness mattered.

CHAPTER 23

In Retrospect

Before I had my stroke, the only kind of books I read were textbooks. Now, I read all kinds of books: mysteries, biographies, histories, fiction, and self-improvement. I realize the stroke has had a direct impact on my communication (speech, writing, and overall comprehension), but it came back . . . not all of it, but I am a far cry from where I was in those first years after the stroke.

I remember one time, not too long after my stroke, I was sitting on my bed with Kelly. I was reading about neurobic exercises from the book *Keep Your Brain Alive* by Lawrence Katz. It had so many pages that I couldn't understand. I didn't know the words. I didn't know what they meant. I know now, but that moment still lives with me. I'm not a dictionary geek, but I'm always checking words and idioms, even today—always rebuilding and expanding my vocabulary and improving my fluency.

Four or five months later, I tried to read that book a second time. I could understand 40 to 50 percent, but I had to go very slowly. I went back to it after two years, and I understood a lot more.

When I put that first strategy report together for RIC, I had to do some presentations with a small group of people. They waited until the end and then asked questions. The first question was, "Of all the rehab activities you did, Ted, including speech therapists, physical trainers, doctors, neurologists, alternative medicines, psychologists, acupuncturists, and so on, which one was the most beneficial for you to come back into society?"

I couldn't answer. There was no one thing, no single, primary focus. I told them, "It's like osmosis—it just happens, gradually. You can feel it. You'll know when your abilities come back. I discovered abilities I didn't know I had before my stroke. I've done so many things. People at various times have told me to just do this or focus on that. But I had to know the rationale before I would focus on or do a particular task. When that explanation wasn't provided, I chose a different way. I always had, and still have, strategies and options in place. I had so many things I could do, and I did as many of them as I could. There was always a purpose and a desired result for each. I always kept plugging on. So, maybe the most beneficial things were persistence and resilience."

My comprehension is drastically improved, and that didn't come only from reading. It came from everything I did, because it all impacted my brain, increased my pathways. All of it made a difference. The parts-of-speech class, the ESL teacher, the Northwestern and SDSU experiments, the Aphasia Club, UMAP, participating in the Chicago Archeworks program, working out, Pilates, boxing, and running, and on and on. It was the daily routine of pushing myself mentally and physically.

And not to forget, I had an amazing family and support system behind me. Kelly was always there, supporting me. My family and friends called me and checked in to see how my progress was coming along. They never gave up on my recovery, nor did they ever treat me as if I were lost, and because of that, I never *felt* lost.

I can't tell you the most important component, but none of it would have worked without a positive attitude. You must stay positive.

Determination. Motivation. Tenacity. Perseverance. Persistence. Being Relentless. Don't get yourself down if things don't go your way. Keep trying to retool your approach; you'll find a way to solve a problem and get yourself past any frustrations and rejections you had. Realize that these are providing valuable opportunities to learn for the next time.

Tom

Before the stroke, Ted was all business. Very serious. Since he's recovered, he's got such a sense of humor. He's come almost 180 degrees now. He's so much funnier, and all his humor—his dry sense of humor—has come out. It never came out before the stroke. He's a different person now. I don't know that it's so much for the better, but it seems like a big burden was lifted off his back. He's become a real person now. He's not a robot who was doomed to work relentlessly every day. He's just funny. He's funny to be with. And we're just as close as we were before the stroke—probably closer.

I'm not embarrassed to say this: The majority of younger brothers would look up to their older brother, right? Ted would always look up to me. But now, despite being eleven years older than him, I look up to him. He just has this power. When we go out, he makes all the decisions, and I don't have any problems with that. I'll meet him in Las Vegas at eleven on a Friday night, which is really two a.m. my time, and he'll say, "Come on, let's go out to dinner." I'm so tired from traveling all day, but I think nothing of going out to dinner with him because he asked me to meet him.

I'd do anything in the world for him. I really would. I'm the oldest of five boys and a girl, and our relationships are good between everybody. But, between me and Teddy, it's just something . . . special.

He didn't pay me to say that, either.

\- - -

In July 2012, two and a half years after I moved to California, I did a short PowerPoint presentation at Chapman University in Orange, California. I put together a succinct summation of what happened to me in Chicago, big pauses for me to think, and how I had amplified my own rehab so that I always felt comfortable and in charge of my recovery. It was a big moment for me, but it's not the end of my story. It's only the beginning of a new chapter of my life.

I've wondered sometimes, throughout the few years after my stroke, what would have happened if I hadn't had a stroke. Would I still work in the financial industry? I really enjoyed it, but I spent countless hours driving my career, at the cost of having real fun and deeper relationships with my family, my friends, my wife. I could have continued to hone my financial and people skills, attained my objective of being a CFO for one of the premier hedge funds in the world, managed a group of people, contributed to the largest global institutions, and worked with world-renowned financial experts.

But now, I help people who need more support. I feel such gratification in giving back to society. It gives me pleasure to know that I can motivate people and give them hope, even when they've experienced a life-changing health crisis. I'm always learning and educating myself on the medical aspects of strokes and aphasia. I enjoy seeing my family and friends more than I ever did before. I try different things that I would never have had the chance to do. I learned to play and enjoy golf, joined book clubs, immersed myself in the world of art, made some great friends, and I am still meeting new faces.

I am more aware of things around me. I know myself and my identity better than before. During my recovery, I focused on hearing what others had to say, especially when my speaking was dormant. I've become an excellent listener, especially at times when I experience anxiety and stress, when my speech is not so fluent.

Yes—I'm having fun more than before my stroke. And that is doing a world of good for me. I've created a new, better blueprint for my life. I am blessed to have the chance to have a fresh start.

My story is still being written, in a sense. I'm speaking in more places to spread the word about my experiences, the power of determination, and the possibility to change the patterns in our lives. I have a totally different perspective on life, a completely different way of going through my days, weeks, months, and years. I'm engaged in *living*, instead of in work.

Life is not a sprint, but a journey that is meant to be fully enjoyed.

Epilogue

The trick to getting through the hardest times in life is to remember that there are many roadblocks along the way, but often, when you conquer those obstacles, there is greater happiness awaiting you on the other side.

After living in California, on my own for a while, I was ready to begin dating again. I had friends who were supportive during that time in my life. Ultimately, it was one of those friends who suggested a blind date. As most would, I hesitated before agreeing. At this point, I had been through so much, so many awkward, difficult moments, I knew that I could survive even the worst blind date. So I finally agreed to go.

"Good evening, Michelle. This is Ted," I said that day, letting her know that I had gotten her number from our mutual friend. I was quick to suggest that we should meet in person. "I'm not interrupting your dinner or anything, am I?"

"Well, actually," she responded, "it's not really evening here. It's nearly ten o'clock." This was followed by a lighthearted laugh. "I'm going to be in New York City for the next three months," she added. I had been told by our friend that she was working in film production. "You could always come here to see me," she suggested, but it was clear that she doubted I would agree to do so. She didn't know, yet, that my family still lived in New York. I hadn't realized that she was raised as an East Coaster too.

Two weeks later, I took a gamble that would ultimately lead to a big payoff. I boarded the plane and landed in New York City not long before we were scheduled to meet for a sushi dinner at Blue Ribbon, in Soho. Of course, I also contacted some of my family members to see if they had anything planned that week and if they could visit.

Typically, a first date—especially a blind date—would be awkward, but Michelle and I had been talking on the phone for two weeks at that point. Each of our phone calls had stretched for nearly an hour. I already knew about her job and about how she valued her family, her education, and her friends immensely. There was one big thing that she didn't know about me, though.

"I had a stroke several years ago," I told her, dropping it as naturally as possible into our dinner conversation. We'd been at the restaurant, enjoying sushi and sake, for a while. She later told me that she thought the alcohol was to blame for the slight slur in my speech, but I took the time to explain, briefly, all that I had been through to recover my speech and my physical abilities. I didn't go too in depth, though. It wasn't the time to get into how influential aphasia had been in my life. I waited until the third date for that. Surely, that's what they mean by the "third-date rule."

When she laughed at that joke and others like it, I knew that we'd be going on many more dates together. This was the first person in a long while with whom I felt so comfortable. No matter what we did or where we were, we managed to find reasons to laugh together. At home, in the quiet of my apartment or hers, we would sit together on the couch and watch television, simply enjoying the moments of peace. *Breaking Bad* quickly became a favorite show of ours, and one that we would discuss, even when we couldn't be together and even when we were hundreds of miles apart.

One day we were talking on the phone while she was working on location on a film project in New Mexico. "Come see me," she said. We knew that if I didn't go to her, we wouldn't see each other for several weeks, so I jumped on another plane. She was even more excited to see me than usual. She had a surprise up her sleeve. "You know, they shoot *Breaking Bad* just down the road," she said with a suggestive smile.

I laughed, "Oh yeah?"

"Yeah. I was thinking we could go grab a quick Tex Mex dinner and drive by. What do you think?" I thought it was a great suggestion and smiled broadly at her surprise. We drove by the house that evening, but apparently, we weren't the first to think of doing so. Someone from the house came out to the road and wrote down our license plate number. We looked at each other and laughed, both imagining a call from the police regarding our new stalker status and decided that we might as well get something out of it. So, we jumped out of the car and took some selfies in front of the house.

That is the beautiful part about being with Michelle; we always manage to find fun wherever we go, spontaneity. I've talked with her about my past, the stroke, and the aphasia. With other new people, there would be some awkward moments, but with Michelle, that awkwardness never existed. She seems to be able to read my mind, even when I can't get my thought out. She understands me in a way that others never did. We've traveled a lot, from the start of our relationship. A lot of the travel was because of her job, but we also visited friends and family. On one of those trips, we decided to stay with her parents, which worked out to my benefit.

"Michelle, you should show your mom some of the features of her new car," I said to her.

"Ted, it's nine thirty at night," she said. "I can show her in the morning."

"Oh, but she'll love it," I responded, eager to get her to leave the house for a few minutes. Then, I turned the plea to her mother. "You won't believe all of the features these new cars have now. The technology is incredible."

"Ted, it's 12 degrees out," Michelle started.

"That's okay," her mother said. "We'll just go out for a minute. I'd love to see it." Michelle just looked from her mom to me and back again, then shrugged her shoulders and picked up her jacket.

I knew they wouldn't last long in the dark of night and with it being so bitter cold. As soon as the door closed behind them, I turned to her father.

I had gotten to know her parents fairly well by this point, and I was excited to broach this idea to her father of me marrying his daughter soon. I dove in and admitted that I had fallen in love with Michelle, that I didn't want to take the chance of ever losing her, and asked for his blessing should she agree to be my wife. Although I had strongly suspected that he would happily agree, it was still a relief when he smiled and spoke his consent just as the door opened again. That night, I did my best to contain my happiness and excitement so I wouldn't give anything away.

On the following trip to New York City for the Thanksgiving holiday, Michelle started to feel a bit ill.

"Ted, I'm not feeling very well. I think I'd rather stay in for the night," she told me.

"Let's just go get some dinner. I made reservations at Gotham Bar and Grill." I could tell that she didn't feel up to going, but it was important that she did. She was even more shocked when I ordered an abundance of food and drinks—oysters, French wine, truffle pasta, and more.

"Ted, are you sure that you really want to order all of that? I'm not very hungry. I'm still feeling a little off," she kept saying. I assured her that I was hungry enough. When the food came, despite her cold, she couldn't resist. It was delicious. I smiled at her when the waiter had cleared the plates away. She smiled in return.

"What would you do, Michelle, if I asked you to marry me?"

She rolled her eyes. "Really? You have to ask what my answer would be after all of this time?" I couldn't help but laugh at that before pulling the ring from my pocket.

"Michelle, will you do me the honor of being my wife?" Her smile grew and she laughed a little.

"Of course! Yes!"

Then I kissed her. She couldn't believe that I had the ring with me the entire time.

There was a group of people seated close enough to have over-heard the whole exchange. "Was that the proposal?" one of them asked with a chuckle.

Michelle happily laughed back. "It was."

"Did you say yes?"

"Of course I did," she responded with a big smile. The guy laughed and his whole group offered up a series of "Congratulations!"

Not far behind this, the maître d', whom I had come to know well on previous business engagements I attended at Gotham, came over to offer his congratulations as well. And behind him was a waiter car-rying a cake in honor of Michelle agreeing to marry me.

Perhaps it made her feel better, or made her forget the cold, because after that, we sat and enjoyed dessert and drinks and spoke about our future.

"How do you think your mom will respond?" I asked, laughing, though I already knew her answer. She laughed again. She was soon turning forty and had lived the single life throughout her twenties and thirties. We both knew that both of her parents would be more than happy to hear that she was going to settle down. "My mom? You're more worried about her reaction than my dad's?"

"Well, yes. I already asked his permission."

"What? When?"

"While you were showing the new features of her new car to her," I answered and then watched as the realization crossed her face.

"That's why you wanted me to show her the car in the dark, in freezing cold temperatures?"

I just laughed in response. And, when I later told my brothers and sister, they all showed excitement. My life was moving forward. Michelle made me feel complete. Well, almost complete . . .

We hadn't been engaged for long when we decided that we were missing something—not between us, but rather we were ready to share something. I asked her to move in with me, and she gave up her West Hollywood apartment. When we had settled on a house together, we moved in and started yet another search—the hunt was on for the perfect pet. The title went to an adorable Pomsky (a combination of a husky and a Pomeranian), which we named Zorro, because his coloring made it look as though he were wearing the mask of Zorro. Our life was truly beginning to feel full as we welcomed the adorable, funny, cuddly fur baby into our home.

At some point, though, we knew that we were going to have to deal with planning a wedding. Initially, we thought about eloping or just having our families and a few friends over to the house for an intimate ceremony. However, as we talked more about what we wanted to do after the wedding, it became clear that it might be best to combine the wedding, reception, and honeymoon into a fantastic trip overseas.

She asked about my heritage, and that led to us discovering that neither of us had ever been to Scotland. Arrangements were made for a trip to scout the castles in the country of my ancestors. A relative of a friend was able to help us narrow our search before we left the United States. When we arrived and saw them in person, there was no question in our minds. We both fell in love with Borthwick Castle, a fifteenth-century, well-maintained, historically pertinent castle kept in near-original state. There were no elevators, the doorways were small and rounded, and one could even tour the dungeons in its cellars. It was authentic. It made us feel as though we had fallen into an episode of another of our favorite shows, *Game of Thrones*. Although it wasn't really the set of *Game of Thrones*, it had once housed Mary, Queen of Scots. It was beautiful. It was the perfect site for a May wedding.

Just before Memorial Day, we made the return trip to Borthwick Castle, in Edinburgh, Scotland. On the 28th of May, we were wed before forty-five guests—family and friends willing to make the trip overseas to see us united. An owl named Bonnie carried the rings across the chapel and to the arm of the best man. The small pouch carried by Bonnie was removed by the maid of honor, and she handed it to the minister. In the pouch were the rings that would mark the start of our lives as a married couple.

There are challenges in life. Everyone must face obstacles along the way. These can be so large, at times, that they seem to cast a shadow over the light at the end of the tunnel. But if you keep fighting, working hard for what you want most, for what matters most, you may find a brighter light than you ever expected.

There are times when I simply sit in our home alone, watching our puppy run around and reflecting on everything that has taken place since the stroke. I ask myself, "If I had to do it all again, would I do it differently? Would I write a different story for myself?"

The answer to those questions are always the same. I wouldn't change anything! There were many obstacles, a lot of ups and downs, and a lot of effort was required to conquer them, but now I am bearing the fruits of my labor, while still being able to give back to the people who need it most.

Acknowledgments

I would like to express my sincere gratitude to everyone who supported me through these trying times and my recovery.

My Family . . .

It is so important to have your family around you in times like this for support. I look at them now through a different lens. My family was and is always there for me—more than ever. It is hard to describe how my family took the news. They knew the stroke was serious and terrible, and they knew they should be with me physically during this crisis. And they all came to give me support when I needed it most. I am so grateful and lucky to have brothers and a sister like them. Thank you for your support.

I would like to also thank all my other relatives for supporting me.

Tom, Jeannette, Gina
Gary, Nancy, Kristine, Gary Jr., Kyle
Jeff, Linda, Jonathan, Jennifer
Scott, Karen, Scotty Jr., Bobby, Timmy
Nancy, Danny, Danny Jr.

Special Thanks ...

I want to thank Kelly, who supported me, encouraged me, and had the patience to help me get over my stroke, surgeries, and the rehabilitation thereafter. She endured the sadness, frustrations, and worries of my condition. I am grateful for having someone of this stature supporting me, being tolerant with me, and helping me fight through this terrible event. I'm glad she is still my close friend.

My Friends ...

These are the people who stuck with me through these trying times. It was difficult for me to thank them when I couldn't talk to them or comprehend what they were saying. Merely having them there or sending cards and emails was so critical for me. I didn't realize it until later, but having friends like this played a major part in my rehabilitation.

I read all the cards and emails that were sent to Kelly and me by friends and family when they learned that I'd had a massive stroke. They kept in contact with Kelly to see how the process was going. It was unbelievable that all the people listed below provided support for Kelly and me.

Tony Mauro	Sayuri Yuzaki
Paul Horowitz	Dean and Vivian Stephan
Doug and Luanne Butler	Dick and Marty Casolari
Christine, Molly, and Trey Davis	Linda Mitchell
Andrew and Vicky Robinson	Patti Stasny
Beth Bonnani-Leyser	Barbara Horne
Dan and Sue Restmeyer	Scott Bryant
Gerald Beeson	Greg Soueid
Adam Cooper	Adam Greissman
Dave Syverson	Andy Narayan
Todd Monti	Lee Tate
Naomi Ietsune	Shoko Chiba

Steve Greenblatt

Rich Reynolds

Ravi Iyer

Lee Knight

Mike and Linda
Salzberg

Mark Austen

Austin McClintock

Chris Yost

Jay and Itsuko
Beddow

Michael Bambo

Juan Pujadas

Valerie Brami

Luke Wimer

David Doerfer

Roger White

Trevor Hill

Raymond
Krawczykowski

Anthony Venezia

Kenji Watanabe

Dan DiFilippo

Yasuko Murozono

Ken Griffin

Rebecca Fuller

Trish Gilbert

Paul Hamill

Cathy LoPiccolo

Colleen Greenrod

Ginin Baikie

Thomas King

Kai Lin

Matt Betourney

Tony Fox

Aspen Antonio

Ryan Mersman

Ruth Collard Sotak

Brian Dodson

Bertan Yew

Bridget Malone

Sarah Shoreman

Amy Huber

Erica Nelson

Eoin O'Shea

Kathy Chapman

Anthony Power

Paul Pensa

Marc Adam

Nigel Walder

Robert Stevens

Nigel Bretton

Neil Purvis

Mark Stafford

Helen Taylor

Pam Konops

Tom Zingalli

Richard Rodeschini

Doreen D'Agostino

Nigel Wright

G. W. Hong

Gallie Oliver

Philip Tye

Seymour Kessel

Dave Fisher

Charles Bain

Steve Atkinson

Ewa Kerin

Dan Raimondi

Paul O'Keefe

Simon and Shiralee
Lloyd-Jones

Suzanne and Wayne
Schell

The Casolari Family

Kirsten McElroy

Arlene, Tom, and
Thomas Yamond

The Rieders

Tina Pavone

Pat and Bob Drew

Lisa Moss

Jim and Liz Watson

Jeff and Melissa Ross

Georgia and Phil de
Roziere

Tracey and Rick Sears

Cindy and Jeff
Yingling

Pat and Bob
McMenamin

I'm sure there are many other emails Kelly and I received, so I offer my heartfelt thanks to those who also supported and comforted us.

These are my doctors, therapists, and friends who guided me through my rehabilitation:

Jesse Taber, Terence Sullivan, Doreen Kelly Izaguirre, Leora Cherney, Barry Schaye, Dan Goffman, Sherrie Malleis, Kyla Garibaldi, Belma Hadziselimovic, Patrick Byrne, Leigh Chethik, Steve Small, Audrey Holland, Sarah Houseman, Jamie Herbst, Jaime Lee, Anne Armstrong, Leann Schouten, Joy Fried, Annie Kennedy, Joanne Pierson, Sharron Turner, Edie Babbitt, Janet O'Connor, Tracy Love, Michelle Ferrill, Richard Harvey, Vivek Jain, Roberta Elman, Alan Kanter, Peter Blake, Tim Miner, Wes Bell, Julio Yarzagaray, and my colleagues from Archeworks.

These are the aphasia programs that strongly supported my efforts to speak again:

Rehabilitation Institute of Chicago, Northwestern University, University of Michigan Aphasia Program, Adler Center of Aphasia, Toronto Aphasia Education, San Diego State University, University of California-Irvine.

A New Chapter in My Life . . .

I have reached a point at which recovery is no longer the most important piece of my day. I am now free to enjoy the new life that I have built in California. To my beautiful wife, Michelle Thomas-Baxter. Her support, encouragement, smile, and quiet patience keep me going. Words cannot describe how lucky I am to have her in my life. I love her and look forward to our lifelong journey.

How I Did It: The Techniques and Activities That Led to My Post-Stroke Recovery

Year One: 2005

REHABILITATION INSTITUTE OF CHICAGO (RIC IN THE CITY)

- Learned how to walk again as an inpatient
- Learned to stand from a wheelchair
- Walked ten steps, then twenty steps, adding ten each time until I could string together one hundred steps
- Walked reliably after seven months
- Participated in physical therapy as an outpatient three times a week for six weeks
- Used a workbook to begin to recover my speaking abilities
- Began basic aphasia therapy with Melissa Purvis

RIC NORTHBROOK

- Entered outpatient speech and physical recovery rehab program for two months
- Socialized on my own initiative with people who had different disabilities

- Solved crossword puzzles and jumbles
- Incorporated exercises on my own, such as leg machine workouts and balancing on an exercise ball
- Used a basketball, practiced layups to put the ball in the hoop
- Progressed from walking to running

UNIVERSITY OF MICHIGAN APHASIA PROGRAM

- Took part in immersive speech therapy eight hours a day, five days a week, for six weeks (with fifteen other individuals who had aphasia)
- Obtained and studied the *Oxford Picture Dictionary* by Norma Shapiro and Jayme Adelson-Goldstein
- Learned and tried to retain nouns, tried to add verbs for common activities
- Created a script of basic nouns and verbs that I could use to get around town
- Measured progress via tests from therapists and interactions with others
- Continued working with weights and running on a treadmill (using YMCA facility)

NORTHWESTERN UNIVERSITY (EVANSTON)

- Participated in research and experiments
- Worked in both one-on-one therapy sessions and group sessions with three or four other patients
- Read books and was prepared to answer therapists' questions
- Continued to measure progress with tests from therapists

Year Two: 2006

RIC IN THE CITY

- Participated in aphasia experiments testing retention and intonation
- Entered the Aphasia Club

- Read books and discussed them with other stroke survivors in a therapist-led group

ATTENDED PRIVATE FOUR-WEEK APHASIA THERAPY IN ORLANDO, FLORIDA

- Participated with another male individual with aphasia
- Participated in conversational therapy
- Practiced my speech using three different games

PRIVATE THERAPY

- Added a student therapist from Northwestern University
- Added another private therapist, Doreen Kelly Izaguirre, to concentrate on conversational techniques

PERSONAL PLAN

- Purchased and used language workbooks on my own for one to two hours each day
- Learned new words from flash cards for kindergarten through second grade
- Used computer programs and software from Earobics, Bungalow, Parrot to learn to form vowels and improve my articulation by mimicking the example on the screen
- Learned how to put sentences together
- Joined a gym (Crunch Fitness) to use the treadmill for jogging and eventually running; used a personal trainer to use basic weights and to learn how to box

Year Three: 2007

ARCHEWORKS

- Entered in an eight-week mini Archeworks summer program
- Participated in the team that designed, built, and implemented a movable stage
- Entered a one-year program in education and public

community for Chicago communities that was a partnership between RIC and Archeworks

- Took ethics and morals courses
- Developed and gave four presentations for large groups
- Used social and conversational skills to complete project with Starbucks

NORTHWESTERN UNIVERSITY

- Participated in a vocabulary intensive program for five months
- Watched CNN clips and summarized and wrote about each clip in three sentences and then spoke about it with the therapist

PERSONAL PLAN

- Began using the dictionary to add words to my vocabulary each day
- Added idioms to my daily speech
- Continued reading books
- Acupuncture—three times a week
- Psychiatrist—once a week

RIC IN THE CITY

- Participated in the golf program (play golf once a week)
- Practiced my golf swing at the golf range to improve balance, physical skills

Year Four: 2008

PERSONAL PLAN

- Enrolled in an English program at the Feltre School to learn the language and learn to write stories
- Sought out an English as a Second Language instructor from Loyola University

- Designed an ideal aphasia program for stroke survivors as a strategic planning exercise
- Reduced acupuncture to once a week
- Researched aphasia-related nutrition to find foods that helped my fluency, memory, comprehension like blueberries, pineapples, and caffeine in coffee
- Decided not to pursue some recovery avenues, such as using a hyperbaric chamber or learning to sing

Year Five: 2009 and After

PERSONAL PLAN

- Gave more presentations to continue improving my articulation and fluency with the goal of becoming a public speaker
- Met with stroke survivors to help them and to socialize

PLANNED A MOVE TO NEWPORT BEACH, CALIFORNIA, ON MY OWN

STARTED AT THE THERAPY CLINIC AT SAN DIEGO STATE UNIVERSITY

- Entered a new book club at SDSU
- Participated in aphasia research at SDSU and had one-on-one therapy

PURSUE VOLUNTEER PROGRAMS, BOARD MEMBERSHIP, AND PHILANTHROPIC OPPORTUNITIES

- University of California, Irvine (hospital and campus)
- St. Jude's Hospital
- Hoag Hospital
- American Heart and Stroke Association
- Laguna Art Museum
- Laguna College of Art and Design

Sample of Therapy Exercises

A ll my therapists from top-flight programs gave me grammar exercises. Going through all these exercises, which were from kindergarten to college SAT level, helped me get better. But, it was slow and tedious.

It was interesting to watch the levels of grammar, articles of speech, and even the choice of words get better and better each year, but I had to study!

To me, it was starting from scratch, from the kindergarten level—which, at that point, I learned nouns. From there, I learned about different words that meant the same concept, the articles of speech, simple sentences, complex sentences, putting different concepts in a single sentence, etc.

These are examples of exercises I had from various programs I had across the United States (e.g., University of Michigan Aphasia Program, Chicago Rehabilitation Institute of Chicago, Northwestern University, San Diego State University, private therapists):

EXERCISE 1: PICTURE OF NOUNS

Food	Hamburger	Pizza	Burrito	Spaghetti
Bread	Cheese	French Fries	Hot Dog	Popcorn
Fruit	Banana	Ice Cream	Cookie	Candy
Drink	Water	Juice	Soft Drink	Coffee

EXERCISE 2

I used language index flash cards obtained from a bookstore, and I progressively got better, from grade-school to college level.

I can't quite explain why, but if you simply read through each card three times a day, you will be amazed at what you pick up.

Skill Area: Language
Ages: 5 through 12
Grades: K through 7

EXAMPLE 1

A flash card that has:
"Who was the main actor in *Mission Impossible*?"
Answer on other side: Tom Cruise

EXAMPLE 2

A flash card that has:

"Who was Magellan?"

Answer on other side: A Portuguese explorer who led the first expedition that sailed around the earth

EXERCISE 3

Tell the story of this family in the picture:

EXERCISE 4

I learned, reviewed, and repeated numerous exercises that seem very simple, but they weren't at that point—as a person who just had a stroke and now has aphasia.

Simple exercises like this:

SUBJECT (WHO?)	VERB (WHAT?)	LOCATION (WHERE?)	TIME (WHEN?)
I	1) Eat 2) Ate 3) Will Eat (Breakfast, Lunch, Dinner)	at home	Monday
My family	1) Watch TV 2) Watched TV 3) Will Watch TV	in New York	This Weekend
My friend	1) Go 2) Went 3) Will Go (Shopping)	at the store	Saturday
The man	1) Work Out 2) Worked Out 3) Will Work Out	at the gym	At Night

EXERCISE 5: THE "BIBLE" OF LEARNING THE TYPES OF WORDS

The Oxford Picture Dictionary
by Norma Shapiro and Jayme Adelson-Goldstein

An example of the contents:

Everyday Language

- A Classroom
- Personal Information
- School
- Studying
- Everyday Conversation
- The Telephone
- Weather
- Describing Things
- Colors
- Prepositions
- Numbers and Measurements
- Time
- The Calendar
- Money
- Shopping

EXERCISE 6: SPEECH SCRIPTS (SAMPLES I USED FROM REHABILITATION INSTITUTE OF CHICAGO)

- Try to memorize the words, helps conversation: tone and the content
- Try to memorize the key points which I have put in the right margin

TALKING STOCKS

You: Nice to meet you. Are you from New York originally?
Mary: Oh no. I moved here from Boston. I transferred jobs.

Try to remember: New York originally

You: What type of work do you do?
Mary: I work at Citicorp in the mortgage loan department.

Try to remember: Type of work do you do

You: Oh, I used to be with Citicorp Investment Bank. So, what are interest rates like these days?
Mary: Well, we're waiting to hear what Bernanke is gonna say next.

Try to remember: Citicorp Investment, Interest rates like these days

You: Do you follow the stock market for your line of work?
Mary: Not for work, but personally I do.

Try to remember: Stock market for line of work

You: What kinds of stocks have you invested in? I've got some tech, some utilities, and also health care. I think I'm well diversified.
Mary: Sounds like you've tried to spread it out.

Try to remember: Kind of stocks—tech/utilities/health care, diversified

You: Yes, if one area tanks, you've got money somewhere else. Then, I can take more risks with my money.

Mary: Hmmm . . . I think I should talk to my broker.

Try to remember: Area tanks, got money somewhere else

You: The idea is diversification. I think you might consider diversifying your portfolio. Your broker will discuss this with you.

Mary: It doesn't seem like stocks have been moving much lately.

Try to remember: Diversification

You: Yeah, that's true. Well, it was nice talking to you. I've gotta run.

Mary: Okay, bye.

Try to remember: Nice talking

Questions for Discussion

How did Ted's drive and determination aid in his recovery?

What are some facts about stroke recovery you learned from reading this book? Do you feel more aware of the symptoms of a stroke? Do you think you are better able to take action in a situation such as Ted and Kelly's?

Do you know anyone who has suffered a stroke or other traumatic brain injury? How has their recovery compared to Ted's? How has your relationship with them been affected by the injury? Does reading this book make you want to change how you interact with them?

Discuss the role relationships play in Ted's recovery (e.g., speech therapists, caregiver, wife, friends, family members, neurologists).

Has reading Ted's story made you want to change the way you live your life?

A major goal of Ted's recovery is to give back. What are some things you could do to give back to the community and stroke survivors?

Has reading this book increased your awareness of aphasia? Has it changed the way you might react to someone you meet with a speech impediment?

How has reading Ted's story made you appreciate the little things we take for granted, like ordering coffee at Starbucks or speaking to a stranger in the street?

What are some of the things that Ted did in his recovery that you would consider doing yourself after experiencing an incident like a stroke or traumatic brain injury to help your recovery?

Who can benefit from reading this book aside from stroke survivors?

Why did Ted try activities like art to aid in his recovery? Do you think that using a vocation like art (e.g., joining a museum or taking an art class) helps with stroke recovery?

Ted eventually joined a book club for stroke survivors. How important was this to his speech recovery?

Do you know the difference between the features of your right brain and your left brain? Which side of Ted's brain was more affected after he experienced the stroke? How did he overcome this to be able to reintegrate into society?

Does Ted see himself as completely recovered?

How did Ted prevent himself from going into a deep depression after his stroke?

Which passage in *Relentless* that describes Ted accepting his aphasia and making the decision to deal with it stood out to you the most?

How has this book changed the way you would you deal with aphasia both personally and with the people in the world who have it?

Discuss the role that independence plays in Ted's story.

When Ted was an inpatient at Rehab of Chicago, he figured out when no one was watching—between the nurses' shifts—so that he could try to walk by himself. Why was he so obsessed with getting himself out of bed and trying to walk when no one else was around?

Author Q&A

Q: What was your writing process like for this book? How did your aphasia affect your ability to write and what are some ways you overcame it?

A: When I just started the process of writing a memoir, which was about four to five years ago, my writing was below average, and because of that, I almost stopped. I had to really think about how I could get my ideas and thoughts from my brain onto paper. I had to put those ideas into sentences and then into a draft of the manuscript.

When I first had the idea to write a memoir, I knew I would need a ghostwriter to help. I used a dictionary and English usage texts to help me as well. And my comprehension of what I experienced when I had the stroke and my recovery became clearer every year. As I moved forward with the project, I noticed that each year my writing improved, and I continued to practice. So eventually, I overcame the aphasia factor.

Q: Were there any times you seriously considered giving up during your recovery?
A: Yes, after Kelly introduced the golf teacher to me when we went

to Scottsdale for a vacation of sorts and also during several stages of rehab. I would practice my golf swing and couldn't do anything to hit the ball beyond ten or twenty yards. It was so frustrating, and it wasn't because I didn't have my strength back or I didn't know the sport of golf; it was my coordination and taking my time and keeping a calm presence— it had to do with all of the little things that go into making a fluid swing and hitting the ball.

Q: What was more difficult for you—the physical or mental parts of recovery?
A: The mental parts of recovery were the hardest.

I had to succumb to the fact that I have aphasia, and with that there are limitations. Once I accepted that, speech and talking became easier. It was very slow at first, but I could see that achievements could be made.

Q: What do you consider to be the most important thing people should know about having a stroke or stroke recovery?
A: Just know that you cannot give up. There are many options that you can take to help you get better. And practice, practice, practice, even when you want to quit or give up or it looks like a bleak or somber situation. Try again the next day or next week or even next month. Keep trying—persistency is key!

Q: In the epilogue, you mention that you wouldn't change the fact that you had a stroke or any other subsequent events in your life, but *if* you could change anything about your life before the stroke would you?
A: In that sense, yes, I would have done a better job communicating with my loved ones, and I would have taken more time to hang out with friends and my family..They would have been more of a priority.

Q: What accomplishment are you most proud of since your stroke?
A: When I went to the program called Archeworks in Chicago, the first time I got up in the front of a small group of listeners (almost

100 people) since I had my stroke and delivered a presentation on our progress. I was nervous and worried that I would mess up before I actually delivered the speech.

Q: What are some things that you still struggle with today? Do you expect to overcome them eventually?

A: I always experience anxiety in some of the situations I am in, which usually means my speech is not as fluent or I miss some of the words that I usually have no trouble with or my sentences are a little off. But I measure myself on my progress from year to year. I always make sure that I am improving from one speech to the next or just in conversation. And I continue to practice.

So, yes, I will eventually overcome my struggles with speech and aphasia.

Q: What kind of therapy was most helpful to you and why do you think this was so?

A: One to one private therapy: We began with verbs and prepositions and how to use them in sentences and then moved to casual conversational speaking. It gave me the opportunity to practice my speech and state my ideas with the same therapist, who I could bond with and form a relationship with. This became someone who really cared about me as a person and was able to give me the necessary attention.

Q: Obviously, your determination played a significant role in your remarkable recovery. Do you think it's possible for others to reach the level of recovery at the speed you did without that same level of determination?

A: Hahaha . . . That's a tough question. I think it would be very tough for a person to achieve the level of recovery that I had without putting determination into the mix. Determination was my bread and butter . . . I woke up every day and made sure that I did something that day to recover my abilities after my stroke. But it really depends on what type of medical incident you've had.

Q: How has your stroke and recovery journey changed your relationships with people—both those close to you and strangers or acquaintances?

A: My relationships with my family have definitely changed for the better. We have become very close. My relationships with old friends and acquaintances have somewhat declined, mainly due to my aspirations now (health, hospitals, and nonprofits), which are different that those of my old friends and acquaintances. I have closer relationships with real friends than before. You realize who your real friends are when they call you just to talk and check on you, even when you can't talk back, which was my situation for a while.

Q: What is the next step for you? Do you have any new projects or goals in mind?

A: I want to continue to help organizations like the American Heart and Stroke Association and health institutions that support causes that relate to stroke rehabilitation and recovery.

Q: The stroke changed pretty much all aspects of your life, but is there anything that hasn't changed?

A: Inside, my will, hard work, and determination haven't changed. I've always enjoyed watching sports, eating great food, and enjoying good movies and plays—this hasn't changed.

About the Author

TED W. BAXTER was born and grew up on Long Island in New York.

He got his bachelor of business administration in three years at Hofstra University in 1984 where he majored in public accountancy. He took a job working for Price Waterhouse as an auditor and he passed all four parts of the CPA exam on the first shot. He then became a management consultant soon thereafter, focusing on financial industry clients. While he was working as a senior manager, he attended the Executive Masters Business Administration program at Wharton on the weekends, where he got his MBA, concentrating on finance and strategy.

He built a financial services consulting practice in Tokyo for Price Waterhouse and rose to partner in record time. For the next six years (1995–2001), he lived in Tokyo and Hong Kong, traveling almost constantly between ten Asia-Pacific countries, first for Price Waterhouse and then as a Credit Suisse First Boston managing director. He left Credit Suisse First Boston, eventually landing the global finance post as a managing director at a premiere hedge fund and investment institution, Citadel Investment Group, based in Chicago.

After spending twenty-two years in the financial industry, he retired as a global finance executive with expertise such as international banks and securities, risk management, financial products, controllership, team-building, change management, strategic planning, and information technology systems.

Ted experienced a massive ischemic stroke in April 2005.

Ted now volunteers his time at two hospitals in Orange County, California, providing his expertise and his experience as a stroke survivor in a communication recovery program and is involved in various philanthropic issues. He also participates as a member of the board of directors of the American Heart and Stroke Association. He does speaking engagements for health-related institutions, hospitals, and universities in California.

Ted lives in Newport Beach, California, with his wife, Michelle, and their dog, Zorro.